WORST INSTINCTS

ALSO BY WENDY KAMINER

Free for All

Sleeping with Extra-Terrestrials

True Love Waits

It's All the Rage

I'm Dysfunctional, You're Dysfunctional

A Fearful Freedom

Women Volunteering

Worst Instincts

COWARDICE, CONFORMITY,
AND THE ACLU

Wendy Kaminer

BEACON PRESS

BOSTON

Beacon Press
25 Beacon Street
Boston, Massachusetts 02108-2892
www.beacon.org

Beacon Press books
are published under the auspices of
the Unitarian Universalist Association of Congregations.

12 11 10 09   8 7 6 5 4 3 2 1

Brief passages of this book appeared in the *Wall Street Journal,*
Free Inquiry, and at The Free For All blog.

This book is printed on acid-free paper that meets the uncoated paper
ANSI/NISO specifications for permanence as revised in 1992.

Text design by Yvonne Tsang at Wilsted & Taylor Publishing Services

Library of Congress Cataloging-in-Publication Data
Kaminer, Wendy.
   Worst instincts : cowardice, conformity, and the ACLU /
      Wendy Kaminer.
      p. cm.
   Includes bibliographical references.
   ISBN-13: 978-0-8070-4430-8 (hardcover : alk. paper)
   1. American Civil Liberties Union.   2. Social groups—Moral and
ethical aspects—United States.   3. Social pressure—United States.
4. Social influence—United States.   5. Kaminer, Wendy.   I. Title.
   JC599.U5K36 2009
   323.06'073—dc22   2008052658

*Materials cited in this book, including records of ACLU meetings, memos, and
correspondence from board and staff members, are available in the Beacon
Press archive at the Andover-Harvard Theological Library, Harvard Divinity
School, Cambridge, Massachusetts.*

*To those honorable, hardworking
ACLU staff members who still
strive to protect civil liberty.*

CONTENTS

Mob Scenes

"Any regrets?" my husband asked my father, an unrepentant atheist on his deathbed at ninety-one. My father paused thoughtfully and said, "Once, I voted for a Republican." We laughed; he paused again and added, "No wait—that wasn't the worst part. The worst part was, I voted for him because he was Jewish."

My father never lost his timing or his mistrust of both religion and tribalism. But despite his intellectual disdain for ethnic solidarity, he'd been tempted by it, to his everlasting chagrin. At least once, his convictions had fallen to the atavistic power of the tribal instinct (which is only exacerbated by historic persecution).

I don't mean to equate tribalism with religion; they converge in Judaism, but not necessarily in other faiths. Indeed, shared religious beliefs can bring people together despite their ethnic differences, just as religious differences can drive apart people with common ethnicities. Tribalism thrives quite apart from religion; an association of atheists can be just as insular and mistrustful of outsiders as any religious group. The tribal instinct is often powerful in groups of people who feel besieged (it's what atheists and beleaguered religious minorities share); but none of us is immune to its temptations. Tribalism is the dark side of associational life.

The vices of association have been exhaustively documented and explained by social psychologists, whose demonstrations of group dynamics (and groupthink) provide valuable empirical evidence for what my mother would have recognized as common sense, and what many of us learn through experience: whether people are brought together by racial, ethnic, religious, social, professional, or ideological affinities, by necessity, accident, or experiment, their intellectual and ethical independence will be tested by the group's authority, their own timidity, and the desire to belong. It's a test that people rarely acknowledge but often fail.[1]

I got an F in moral courage the first time I was tested by my membership in a group. I was in grade school, tagging along with some neighborhood kids who decided to embark on a vicious little prank: we would steal the notebook of a boy we hardly knew, precisely because he guarded it jealously out of fear of being punished for its loss. (He attended a parochial school ruled by reputedly fearsome nuns.) It was nearly fifty years ago, but I still remember hearing the theft proposed, knowing it was very wrong, not voicing my objections, and not even silently walking away. Instead I hung around the edge of the group while others stole and destroyed the notebook. That night, our victim went door-to-door asking if anyone had seen his book; I still cringe at the memory of his appearance at my house and my continued failure to speak up. I knew that I was obliged to speak, so that at least he would know that his notebook was irrevocably lost and its loss was not his fault. But I was simply too ashamed of my conduct to admit it, and my silence only made me more ashamed.

Others may say that I've committed worse crimes since, but I'd disagree. This was an act of gratuitous meanness in which I collaborated because I lacked the courage to dissent or even withdraw. Given the chance, I also lacked the courage to confess. Of course, the theft of a seventh grader's notebook seems to merit no mention compared with the abuses people visit upon each other daily (I don't imagine we caused any lasting harm). But I measure the immorality of our conduct not by its consequences but by its character—mainly, its premeditated, unprovoked maliciousness.

This is not an unusual story: it's repeated whenever individuals are intimidated by the promise and demands of membership into betraying their own ideals, when members are silently complicit in collective wrongdoing, not because they risk violence, imprisonment, or unemployment for speaking up, but because they risk the loss of popularity, if not expulsion from their group. I'm grateful to have experienced the shame of that complicity in childhood; it helped inoculate me against the temptations of belonging, while providing a visceral understanding of the cravenness that enables mobs and, more mundanely, regularly leads groups of people that begin with good intentions to end up acting badly.

Cravenness sometimes begins with a desire to cooperate. Associational life and all its virtues depend on the willingness of individuals to cede the right to act independently, on the basis of independent judgments. The virtues of association are also the source of its vices: Collegiality and an ethic of civility encourage conformity and the suppression of dissent. Group solidarity encourages tribalism. Dedication to mission encourages obedience to people charged with mission control. Loyalty to the group easily subsumes loyalty to the ideals for which the group supposedly stands.

I'm not suggesting that individuals should never compromise their beliefs for the sake of solidarity and the welfare of a collective endeavor. But moral corruption is often incremental, beginning with moral compromises that are rationalized and recast as moral obligations that serve the greater good, while preserving the individual's status in the group. Take this homely hypothetical. Imagine that you're playing golf in a charity tournament and learn that one of your teammates is cheating his way to a victory. If you remain silent, your team wins, and the worthy charity of your choice receives a generous donation. If you reveal his cheating, your team is disqualified, and your charity receives nothing. But another, more deserving team will win, and another charity will benefit, you remind yourself. Your conscience tells you not to win by cheating, but then you consider the social costs and benefits of your choices: Remain silent and you'll join in a victory celebration with your teammates. Speak up and you'll be denounced for ratting out the cheater and betraying the team. You'll never be invited to play with it again. I'd be willing to bet that most people faced with a little dilemma like this would opt for silence and victory, and have little trouble justifying the choice and lying to themselves about their reasons for making it.

The more grievous the offense that leads to victory, the more important victory must seem, in order to rationalize the bad behavior that ensures it. What if your win-at-all-costs teammate sabotages an opposing player and exposes him to harm? What if you know (or have reason to know) that unless someone exposes your teammate's dirty tricks he'll go on playing them? A large majority of people contemplating this hypothetical might imagine themselves exposing the cheater, but in real life I doubt that they would do so. Perhaps some would try to intervene quietly, anonymously, or indirectly to avoid embarrassing the team and being punished for breaking ranks. I suspect that the majority would remain silent, exorcising any pangs of conscience by exaggerating the importance of winning, while minimizing the potential harm, or wrongfulness, of cheating.

The likelihood that members will tolerate and tacitly approve cheating, and turn against one of their number who exposes it, increases if the cheater is team captain or coach. Group survival may depend, or seem to depend, on the agreement of members to follow their leader, whose power may be measured by her success in appearing to embody the group's common purpose or ideals. The more the leader comes to embody the group, the more loyalty or obedience she enjoys, the more her character and competence will determine whether the group's mission is served or eventually subverted by such esprit de corps. Groups naturally fear splintering, and punish disloyalty; counterintuitively, they should also be wary of solidarity, which sometimes breeds corruption and decline. Critical thinking ends when the demonization of dissent begins. You can predict the devolution of a group into a mob when it equates dissent with disloyalty and subjects dissenters to ad hominem attacks on their motives or character, while trivializing or ignoring the merits of their concerns.

I make no general claims here about the moral dispositions of groups or their potential political and personal value, which vary wildly and often unpredictably, of course. I make no general claims about the moral dispositions of dissenters. I'm not advocating for or against association or suggesting that it inevitably entails moral compromise. But membership in almost any group or institution does pose a moral challenge, notably the impulse to minimize or silence disagreement, especially when it involves criticism of the competence or integrity of the group or its leadership. I do hope to illustrate the virtues of dissent, whether or not it's offered by virtuous dissenters. I focus on the challenges of a voluntary association, but similar immorality plays are regularly enacted in government, academia, and business, when majorities acquiesce in obviously unethical conduct. Sometimes the consequences are tragic; sometimes they're trivial or farcical.

The moral equations for individual members differ, according to their roles and status and the mission or business of the group, all of which determine the costs of exposing, criticizing, or complying with malfeasance. Employees asked to engage in conduct they deem unethical have to balance their financial needs and obligations against the dictates of conscience; for them, dissent may be an unaffordable luxury. For members of voluntary associations, informal affinity groups, or not-for-profit boards, however, the practical, quantifiable costs of dissent are relatively low; what they have at stake is their popularity, social status, or the self-respect they derive from identifying with a presumptively righteous group. I'm interested in people who can afford to offer or at least tolerate dissent but who act as if their livelihoods depended on avoiding or suppressing it—rationalizing misconduct or blinding themselves to it, accepting as unquestioned reality their group's idealized vision of itself and silencing critics who point out its fallibility. If belief in the group's virtue calcifies into an article of faith—immutable and not dependent on behavior—then even obviously wrong actions authorized by or for the group are presumed to be right, by virtue of their authorization, and dissenters are heretics, or traitors. Allegiance to the group's self-image becomes an unofficial but avidly enforced requirement of membership.

"America, love it or leave it," self-anointed patriots used to say to Vietnam War protesters. Naturally, dissent is most aggressively denounced when solidarity is most urgently desired—when groups are at war, actually or metaphorically, as our own national history shows.[2] "Your tactics only aid terrorists for they erode our national unity and diminish our resolve," former attorney general John Ashcroft famously warned the Bush administration's critics in 2001. "They give ammunition to America's enemies, and pause to America's friends. They encourage people of good will to remain silent in the face of evil," he concluded, demanding silence from Americans who might disagree with his policies.[3]

At least, in a more or less functioning democracy, dissenters often find support if not strength in numbers: millions of diverse and disputatious Americans constitute a unified group only nominally, symbolically, and in the rhetoric of politicians. In more formal, insular groups or institutions, dissent can be much lonelier and exile much more literal. The dangers of demonizing as well as marginalizing or coolly eliminating dissenters are acute in noncommercial enterprises—advocacy groups, or charitable and religious institutions—that people join and support out of devotion to a cause, in the belief that they're on the side of the angels. When a not-for-profit group idealizes itself, regarding its own rectitude as a fact, not a contingency, it presumes to embody an essential, altruistic, if not sacred, mission, and criticizing the group becomes the equivalent of criticizing or betraying its great cause. Then, members unwilling to leave the group will find ways to love it, rationalizing felonies as well as misdemeanors.

Consider how righteously and routinely princes of the Catholic Church concealed and facilitated the sexual abuse of children by their priests. The decades-long complicity of bishops and cardinals, like the disgraced Bernard Law (now comfortably ensconced at the Vatican) has been exhaustively documented and analyzed.[4] At the risk of oversimplifying this terrible and tawdry scandal, and without dismissing the centuries-old institutional peculiarities that contributed to it, you can imagine how some of these putative moral exemplars might have rationalized their profoundly immoral behavior:

"The Church is the most important institution on earth," I imagine them thinking. "Not only is it devoted to aiding the poor and oppressed, not only does it save lives—it saves souls. Acknowledging the abuse perpetrated by some priests would inflict immeasurable harm on the Church, crippling its capacity to serve. People would die; people would even be damned. Better to address the problem of pedophile priests privately, transferring and treating them, instead of publicly admitting and exposing their crimes."

If the consequences of those crimes are then minimized (as they were by Church officials who were utterly oblivious or willfully blind to the nature and harm of child abuse), while the costs of exposure are maximized, a cover-up appears not just morally acceptable but obligatory. People who share responsibility for the abuse can tell themselves that covering it up is not self-serving cowardice but unselfish service to the Church. Virtue is presumed to lie in protecting the virtuous institution, instead of protecting its individual casualties or remaining true to its ideals.

That's one story these men of God might have told themselves to justify their cover-ups of child molestation. Maybe Church officials concocted different stories offering different justifications for their sins. But it seems likely that the great majority told themselves some exculpatory story or other, engaging in fairly convoluted processes of rationalization. Most of us need to believe in our own essential goodness. When we lie or cheat, we tell ourselves that the lying or cheating is necessary to balance the scale, to remedy or prevent a greater wrong: Think of the embezzler who tells herself that she is only taking what she is owed, that she's long been underpaid and wrongfully denied promotions. Think of the public official who lies about an illegal, covert operation, telling himself that it saved lives and served the nation's interests and that lying was his patriotic duty. Think of the board members of a charity or advocacy group who lie about organizational improprieties, telling themselves that the improprieties were harmless and that acknowledging them would only impair the organization's ability to do good.

It's especially easy to minimize bad behavior by your group if you view it in the context of a good group mission or worse behavior by others. Compared to the atrocities in which people periodically indulge, the quotidian deceits and hypocrisies of organizational life will always seem trivial; and the temptation to view behavior as good enough because it could be a lot worse is always strong. A flexible ethical code offers substantial social advantages, as well as practical benefits. The more demanding and unyielding your own sense of ethics, the more it is apt to aggravate and isolate you, unless you belong to a relatively insular community of like-minded dogmatists. In mixed company, people inclined to moral flagellation are less likely to be valued for their companionship, or membership, than people who forgive their own vices and remain ruefully unsurprised by the absence of virtue in others.

No one likes a scold. Recognizing that not all wrongs are equal, calibrating or rationing moral disapprobation is a necessary exercise of judgment. When people tell themselves that their apparent misconduct, or passive collaboration in the misconduct of others, is in service of a greater good, or simply not that bad, how do we know, how do they know, if they're wrong? Sometimes ethical rules are arguably, justifiably broken. If we can usually agree about the rules, we are bound to disagree often about their application: some will deny what I consider significant ethical infractions, which others will defend as necessary ethical compromises. Absolutists can declare that lying is always wrong, but the rest of us are left arguing about the circumstances that might require or justify a lie. When the Nazis come knocking on your door, it is probably best to lie about the Jew who's hiding in your basement. That's an easy case (with all due respect to Immanuel Kant), because in a murderous, totalitarian regime, truth has either no relationship or an inverse relationship to justice. What if the person hiding in your basement is an immigrant who entered the country illegally, hoping to escape dire poverty? How do you balance your legal responsibilities with your humanitarian impulses? How is your decision affected by your view of the justness of our nation's immigration laws and their adherence to American ideals or the effect of illegal immigration on the nation's welfare?

Philosophers write books about dilemmas like this, involving the classic conflict between individual conscience and collective obligations, and the complicated interdependency of individual and collective purposes or ideals. Outside the realm of philosophy, it's difficult and maybe useless to formulate abstract or categorical rules about the ethical choices and dilemmas posed to individuals by their groups, and I don't intend to try.

My own interest in the conflict between individual conscience and group solidarity didn't begin with abstractions but with my experiences as a dissident member of the American Civil Liberties Union national board. This book focuses on the story, or cautionary tale, of what I regard as a dramatic ethical decline at the ACLU, involving the institutionalization of deceit and abandonment of core civil-liberties principles by staff and lay leadership—enabled by the use of social pressure to silence dissent. Since board members are elected, the soft power of social pressure was supplemented by hard electoral power; members who failed to censor themselves faced formal ejection from the group, not just marginalization. But elections were mechanisms for enforcing norms, not setting them. Criticism of the ACLU would not have been politically treacherous if national and state boards had not willingly fallen in line behind the national leadership, ignoring clear evidence of misconduct.

Following their leaders, ACLU board members engaged in typical organizational behavior—which stood in stark contrast to the ACLU's particular organizational ideals; and that contrast is what makes this tale worth telling. That the impulse to obey and conform can silence and even demonize dissent at the ACLU, an organization avowedly dedicated to protecting dissent, that group identity and solidarity can facilitate secrecy, deceit, and a loss of accountability at the ACLU, a righteous advocate of openness, honesty, and the preservation of accountability in government, are shocking but not surprising truths—testaments to the dangerous allure of belonging, poignant and revelatory of the power human nature exerts over human ideals.

2

The Problem
with Partisanship

Before I begin this account of skullduggery at the ACLU,
I should disclose that many, if not most, prominent ACLU
national staff and lay leaders have denied the truth of my
claims, questioning my character, motives, and emotional
health. I've been called an enemy of the ACLU and an enemy
of civil liberties; without a trace of self-consciousness, some
called me an "enemy within." My willingness to criticize
the ACLU in the press aroused particular ire: along with a
former national board colleague, Michael Meyers, I was the
target of an impeachment campaign (aborted after its public disclosure).[1] I was denounced as "sanctimonious," "self-
centered," "hysterical," "strident," and "shrill," and derided as
a "diva," among other sobriquets. I was referred to, obliquely
but clearly, as a "fucked out boozy bitch," told, obliquely but
clearly, to "fuck off and die," and regularly condemned for
engaging in "uncivil," "ad hominem" attacks because I criticized the conduct and questioned the assertions of ACLU
leadership.

Because my own conduct has been harshly criticized,
because I've been a central combatant in a very heated, internal organizational battle (which I and other dissidents lost),
I lack the advantage of reportorial objectivity in telling this
story. Initially I envisioned my experiences at the ACLU
as the inspiration, not the subject, for a book about ethics,

group dynamics, and dissent, but eventually I found focusing on the ACLU unavoidable. The descent of a civil liberties organization into a soft and unself-conscious authoritarianism provides an eloquent case study in collective perversity. If I'm handicapped by my personal involvement in this story, I'm enabled by intimate, firsthand knowledge of its intricacies. I can't claim objectivity, but I am in possession of an extensive factual record, comprising tapes of meetings, minutes, e-mails, and memos, of which I would welcome careful review.[2]

As I write this, in the summer of 2008, ACLU national executive director Anthony D. Romero enjoys effective control of a compliant national board; he is consolidating control of ACLU state affiliates, which he has had unprecedented power to reward or punish financially, given the ACLU's post-9/11 wealth. (It now boasts hundreds of millions of dollars in assets.) There are good reasons to centralize power at a large, national federation, of course, and good reasons for an executive director and executive committee to control a large board. The ACLU board is particularly unwieldy, comprising eighty-three people, a majority of whom represent state affiliates; thirty members are elected "at large" by their colleagues on the national board and by affiliate boards. The board meets four times a year and necessarily delegates routine governance responsibilities to an eleven-person executive committee and four general counsels, all of whom are board members elected and often reelected by the board for two-year terms. (When I refer to the ACLU leadership, I'm generally referring to the executive director, president, and executive committee, as well as the treasurer and general counsels who serve on the executive committee ex officio.) This is a sensible, democratic electoral system, but like most systems, its integrity depends on the integrity of individual leaders and their accountability to informed, unintimidated followers. As civil libertarians know, the centralization of power inevitability increases the abuse of power, especially when it's unchecked.

Consolidation and corruption of power at the ACLU was

surprisingly swift and met with relatively little resistance from a majority of the board, but it was not peaceful. Beginning in 2003, for a period of about three years, the national board warred over a series of what were either innocent mistakes by Romero or acts of deliberate malfeasance enabled by the executive committee, depending on your point of view. A substantial majority of board members defended and effusively praised the leadership, effectively marginalizing our small group of active dissidents (five to ten people perhaps) and discouraging a larger group of passive supporters from acting up. Our numbers dwindled as people were voted off the board, resigned in disgust or discouragement, or censored themselves in order to stay. (I left the national board in 2006, when my term expired, and I did not run for reelection; I remained on the board of the Massachusetts ACLU.) My colleague Michael Meyers and I were the most hated of Romero's critics—because we engaged in a "vengeful, destructive" campaign against the executive director without any concern for the welfare of the organization, board leaders might say, speaking euphemistically—or, in my view, because we were the most tactless (or direct) and persistent in assailing what we regarded as dishonest, unprincipled conduct (many found us simply obnoxious), and because we were the most willing to criticize Romero and the board leadership publicly, on the record, when dissent was effectively silenced internally and our internal processes for correcting mistakes or misconduct were corrupted. Other board members who spoke to the press tended to speak anonymously or on background.

Many of our battles involved internal governance matters, which aroused relatively little interest, even internally; they included the covert initiation of an extensive donor-research, data-mining program; indications that management was engaged in covert electronic surveillance of staff; wholesale shredding of documents in violation of the organization's document-retention policy (according to the ACLU's former archivist); a proposal to bar board members from criticizing the ACLU (an entirely unnecessary embarrassment, since an informal ban on dissent was enforced by peer pressure and electoral control); allegations that the executive director lied to the board habitually, with the backing of the executive committee; and the routine distribution of misinformation by the national leadership to national and affiliate board members and donors, flatly denying a series of charges that any careful examination of the record (board minutes, e-mails, and other documents) would prove to be true.

Governance matters like these are the business of a board, but they're hardly as compelling as debates about torture, extrajudicial detention, or domestic surveillance, among other post-9/11 concerns. Like many members of not-for-profit boards, ACLU directors generally tend to be less interested in governing the organization than in identifying with its cause; the great majority of board members ignored or denied evidence of the leadership's dishonesty and dismissed other governance controversies as "tempests in teapots" (a favored cliché). Some charged us with lending comfort to the enemies of civil liberty (and naturally reacted with outrage if you compared them with Bush administration partisans who charged administration critics with lending support to terrorists). Others simply stressed the transcendent importance of the ACLU's civil liberties/civil rights agenda and post-9/11 work, which dedicated staff throughout the organization continued to advance. Nationally, for example, the ACLU used the Freedom of Information Act to help expose abuses of the war on terror. It enthusiastically pressed important, high-profile post-9/11 cases, like its legal challenges to Bush administration surveillance programs and 2008 congressional amendments to the Foreign Intelligence Surveillance Act.[3] But occasionally staff members privately protested that quixotic, high-profile initiatives were displacing essential, low-profile work, and they reported being discouraged or prevented from working on cases or controversies unpopular with ACLU members and (especially) major donors, or merely unlikely to inspire substantial contributions.[4]

The ACLU's substantive work was not untouched by misconduct, mismanagement, or mistakes in governance, as many board members wrongly believed. The work was compromised, predictably, by top managers and lay leaders despite the efforts or inclinations of some staff. An organization's effectiveness is not so easily divorced from its integrity, and the ACLU's mission was being quietly transformed, as public relations and fundraising began taking precedence over principle: notably, it retreated from protecting politically incorrect, "offensive" or "hateful" speech and effectively collaborated with what the ACLU officially condemned as a federal blacklisting scheme, rendering fraudulent some of its lucrative, post-9/11 appeals to preserve civil liberty.

A summary of salient facts about our disputes was posted online in the fall of 2006, at Save the ACLU, a Web site (save theaclu.org) launched by a group of about thirty ACLU insiders calling for a change in our national leadership. The Save the ACLU mission statement was brief and general; it lamented the ACLU's failure to practice what it preached, respond honestly to revelations of misconduct, and tolerate internal dissenters; a brief statement of fact accompanied these allegations, substantiated by a voluminous record. The effort was naive: casual ACLU members who had not been involved in what was then a three-year internal dispute would not have known what to make of our charges and would have lacked the time, energy, or sense of urgency needed to investigate them (or read even a small percentage of material posted on the Web site). Many committed ACLU supporters, activists, and allies seemed less concerned with the merits of our claims (if they considered the merits at all) than with the fact that we were questioning the integrity of an organization with which they proudly identified and sharply criticizing its leaders, mainly Anthony Romero, who assumed the office of executive director only days before 9/11, and Nadine Strossen, then in the sixteenth year of her tenure as ACLU president. (She retired in 2008 and was succeeded by Susan Herman, a member of the executive committee since 1992 and reliable Romero protector.)

Denouncing the nation's leading civil liberties organization during a civil liberties crisis wrought by excesses of the war on terror was regarded as treasonous, not surprisingly. (The temptation to close ranks against dissenters is most intense when groups feel under siege.) Criticizing ACLU leaders was equated with criticizing the ACLU. (The leadership had succeeded in embodying the organization.) Criticizing the ACLU was equated with undermining the ACLU, which was equated with undermining civil liberties. (The organization was presumed to embody the mission.) So our motives, not our arguments, continued coming under attack; our charges were summarily dismissed as the sour grapes of vindictive people who had lost power and policy debates. And faster than you might say "loyalty oath," executive directors of ACLU state affiliates were asked to sign letters expressing strong support and admiration for the ACLU national leadership and disdain for the claims of dissidents. (Eighteen affiliate executive directors did so.) At least one major liberal funder urged the leaders of other civil rights and civil liberties groups to join him in a public statement of support for the ACLU leadership.[5] The facts that supported our charges were ignored or met with outright denials, contradicted by an available record that few people ever examined.

If the facts were so convincing, how could they have been so easily ignored? Facts are often overlooked in partisan warfare when loyalty to a team matters much more than the merits of any dispute. Facts are overlooked when they're complicated and voluminous, and understanding them takes time and intellectual energy. (Why take the trouble to examine the facts when you can take the word of leaders in whom you've placed your trust?) Facts are overlooked when acknowledging them is painful, socially disruptive, or requires actions we'd rather not take.[6] Facts are overlooked when they're publicized or confirmed after people have formed opinions and chosen sides.[7] The power of an idée fixe and decline of critical thinking during times of intense partisanship was exemplified in the persistent, mistaken belief that Saddam Hussein was responsible for 9/11, as the Bush administration had repeatedly implied. A 2006 Zogby Poll found that twice as many Republicans as Democrats still believed that "there was a connection between Saddam Hussein and the 9/11 terror attacks" some two years after the 9/11 Commission found no such connection.[8]

ACLU partisans will protest this analogy, deriding what they'll regard as an implicit equation of dysfunction at the ACLU with national political dysfunction during wartime. But I'm equating neither the consequences of public misconceptions about a war with the consequences of members' misconceptions about an advocacy group, nor the importance of relatively honest, national government with the importance of honest associational leadership (although the ACLU's decline loosens an important restraint on government). I am comparing the dynamics of dysfunction and corruption, which are predictably similar: partisanship, tribalism, and other forms of group solidarity discourage critical thinking and attention to facts, whether the group is a social club, a church, an advocacy group, a political party, or a nation, regardless of ideology.

When it encourages people to support actions or ideas they would otherwise oppose, solidarity can be stupefying: "Many are ambivalent, deep inside about the decisions made in the past seven years in the White House," Peggy Noonan wrote in the spring of 2008. "But they've publicly supported it so long they think they . . . support it. They get confused. Late at night they toss and turn in the antique mahogany sleigh bed in the carpeted house in MacLean and try to remember what it is they really do think and what those thoughts imply."[9] When it demands the suppression of dissent, solidarity corrupts. Groups that refuse to entertain doubts about their integrity are bound to lose it.

Partisanship has its virtues, of course: politics is not just the art of compromise; it's also the art of conflict and choosing sides. The problem with partisanship is not so much the conflict it sustains but the misconduct it conceals, the emotionalism it exploits, and the lying it encourages.

3

Not the Crime
but the Cover-up

I

The ACLU began its descent into unethical, unthinking partisanship in 2003, when Executive Director Anthony Romero was accused of concealing information and lying to the board about privacy violations on the ACLU online store, and the resolution of a subsequent investigation by the New York Attorney General's Office initiated in March 2002: a security breach had resulted in publication of personal information about consumers, in violation of the ACLU's privacy policy. A third-party vendor took responsibility for the breach, which was reportedly remedied, but it aroused the interest of the attorney general and was obviously embarrassing for a civil liberties organization committed to policing privacy. Less than a year earlier (in July 2001), the ACLU had complained to the federal trade commission about a similar privacy breach by Eli Lilly.[1]

The ACLU issued a brief press release apologizing for the security breach (which had been discovered by a reporter for *Corporate Legal Times* looking into the ACLU's campaign against Eli Lilly). But Romero did not discuss the privacy violations with the board until the following year (2003), when he mentioned them to the executive committee, after the *Washington Post* reported a second "privacy gaffe."[2] He handled months of negotiations with the New York attorney general in relative secret; then, without consulting counsel, he settled the matter in December 2002 by signing a consent agreement, which he promptly violated. The terms of the agreement explicitly required its distribution to the ACLU board within thirty days; Romero withheld it for some five months. He belatedly circulated it and briefly described the underlying privacy violations at a June 2003 board meeting, under some duress: a staff member, Karen Delince, had discovered the agreement and advised him that he was required to circulate it, citing a provision stating, "The ACLU shall deliver a copy of this [agreement] to all current and future principals, officers, directors, and managers . . . no later than 30 days after the date as of which this [agreement] is executed." Still, Romero continued to insist that he was not obliged to distribute the agreement to the board until Delince put her concerns in writing, prompting him to consult outside counsel, who concurred with her advice. (A few months later Romero would falsely report that he had initiated a staff debate about his obligations under the agreement, after his own careful review of it.) When he finally distributed the agreement to the board in June, he said little about its substance, did not explain that he had violated it, and left some of us with the false impression that it had been negotiated with knowledge of the executive committee and assistance of counsel.

If you're already bored by this very brief summary of a fairly insignificant legal matter (security problems on the ACLU Web site seem to have been remedied), you may sympathize with board members who were content to ignore it, especially in the aftermath of 9/11. But a CEO's failure to disclose information to his board (even to the point of violating a legal agreement) should not be ignored, Yale School of Management professor Jeffrey Sonnenfeld stresses in the *Harvard Business Review*: withholding information undermines the board's ability to govern and initiates a "dangerous, destructive pattern" of mistrust. Effective groups operate in a "virtuous cycle of respect, trust, and candor [that] can be broken at any point," Sonnenfeld observes. "One of the most common breaks occurs when the CEO doesn't trust the board enough to share information."[3] In our case, the CEO seemed not to respect the board enough to share information, as some members privately complained.

Initially, a substantial minority of board members were privately critical of Romero's behavior and his vague, inconsistent excuses for it: when asked to explain his failure to notify the board of his settlement with the attorney general, Romero alternately claimed that he had not focused on the notice provision in the agreement, or that he had not interpreted it to require notice, among other inconsistent explanations. In fact, we learned eventually that he had spent considerable time and money consulting staff and outside counsel about his obligation to notify the board, which made some of us wonder why he didn't simply distribute the agreement, even if he might have had an arguable legal defense for not doing so. Two years later he offered a new explanation to a *New York Magazine* reporter, claiming that he withheld the agreement from board members "to spare them unnecessary paperwork."[4]

Whatever. After reading the agreement in June 2003, board member Marjorie Esman and I expressed concerns about Romero's conduct to the executive committee; in response, we received a chirpy e-mail from board president Nadine Strossen, assuring us that our "process/governance concerns were being addressed by Anthony in the same candid, constructive manner that characterized his presentations to the EC [executive committee] and Board in June. . . . Thanks for your vigilance!" That's when we knew we were in trouble: the executive director would answer our questions about his lack of candor in the same "candid" and "constructive manner" that provoked them. As one board member noted privately to me in an e-mail, after the story of the consent agreement unraveled: "i'm not an attorney so i did not understand 100% of the explanation/discussion at the board meeting where we were informed of the consent agreement, but i do remember being troubled by anthony's body language as he was describing what had happened. now there is an explanation for that."

But like most board members, the author of this e-mail soon rallied round Romero, following the lead of the executive committee. After an unsuccessful effort to persuade the committee to initiate an inquiry into Romero's conduct, I appealed to the full board in September 2003, in a rather lengthy memo, and was promptly chastised by Strossen and other board leaders. A few board members defended me, although more did so in private than in public e-mails (those posted to the full board) or in voice mails. The responses were extreme: My memo was either a "careful exploration and analysis of the issues" or a "shrill one-sided barrage seemingly advancing a position of a sole dissenter in the executive committee." It was either not "organizationally minded" and "a very destructive brief," as well as "hysterical," or it was "very thorough" and "incredibly fair." I was either complicit in a vendetta against Romero ("there have been members of our Board who have a history of trying to undermine Anthony") or "incredibly brave and industrious."

Perhaps predictably, many of the people who began by privately offering me their thanks or support would end by condemning me and other dissidents and even the right to dissent in general. "I agree that this needs a more appropriate airing and I share your concerns about this series of decisions and, sadly, Anthony's hubris more generally. . . . Thank you for your thoughtful and courageous action. Doubtless you are prepared to be misunderstood and unappreciated for your efforts," one board member wrote, in response to my 2003 memo. Some two years later she helped craft a proposal to prohibit ACLU board members from criticizing the ACLU.

Rereading these and other e-mails today, I'm mostly struck by the praise for my "courage" in challenging our organization's leadership. I realize now what I should have realized then: that people who privately regarded my troublemaking as courageous were unlikely to join me in it. They weren't praising my behavior; they were tacitly explaining their hesitancy to support me publicly. I was indeed "industrious," as one board member said (although my industriousness was rather misguided and made little sense strategically). But "brave"? I had nothing at stake except my status in a voluntary association. I was risking nothing that I could not afford to lose. "What are they gonna to do to me," I used to say. "Send me to Guantánamo?"

Rereading my rather extravagant memo about the consent-agreement controversy today, I sympathize with colleagues who thought I was overreacting. "No harm, no foul," they said. The security breach had been remedied; the board had been informed of the privacy violations and the settlement with the attorney general, however belatedly. Romero was relatively new to the ACLU: he had served as executive director a little less than two years when this controversy erupted. He had simply "made a mistake," people declared, urging me and other critics to "move on," comparing our request for an inquiry into his actions and excuses to Ken Starr's investigation of Bill Clinton's sex life.

The analogy was inapt—we were concerned with the conduct of official business—but it was effective. Few board members wanted to take on the unpleasant task of inquiring into Romero's honesty. One leading executive committee member privately told me that he did not want to investigate Romero's handling of the consent agreement because he did not want to have to fire him. Neither I, nor other critics, were demanding Romero's dismissal. I wanted a reason to believe that we could trust him in the future. I wanted an acknowledgment of the truth. But his most ardent defenders on the executive committee apparently feared that investigating and acknowledging the truth of his conduct would inevitability require replacing him. They were the first to raise, and exploit, the possibility of firing Romero—a possibility the board did not want to confront. Instead, it acted on the pretense that the new executive director had made a few innocent mistakes and his critics were "hounding" him out of an excess of prosecutorial zeal or personal animus:

"I do not see 'mismanagement' or 'deception' here," one

of Romero's staunchest defenders on the board explained to me in a private e-mail months later, summarizing the unofficial party line: "I see a 'Golden Boy' who has made relatively few mistakes in his youth, probably covered them up in ways that you or I might not think were the best, and is learning how to deal in an arena that demands more transparency than he is used to. So he makes some mistakes—he is human. Maybe he was caught telling a fib—oh, do I remember my mother teaching me about 'white lies'!"

This willingness to forgive the executive director's "mistakes," along with the effort to cover them up, seems, at first, an arguably reasonable exercise in judgment; but it founders on the final reference to "white lies." Romero's "fibs" were not white lies; that is, they were not offered to spare anyone else's feelings or protect anyone else's status. On the contrary, they were entirely self-serving, and even deflected blame from Romero to a member of his staff.[5] This was the central point that board members had to deny or distort in order to rationalize their executive director's evident misconduct as mistakes. They had to pretend that he was guilty only of telling white lies.

The relative insignificance of the consent agreement made the pretense palatable and developed the board's taste for misinformation, as truths about the leadership's conduct became harder and harder to swallow: board members who initially dismissed Romero's "fibs" about a minor governance issue as harmless errors could not so easily have ignored evidence that he lied to them about betraying a core organizational principle—our opposition to post-9/11 watch lists. But eventually they would ignore and even defend that betrayal, when we found out that Romero had quietly signed a contract with the government promising to use the watch lists to screen employees. By then the board had buried too many truths to begin the process of digging out: board members who believed in their own righteousness (as most people do) would not indict practices they had knowingly enabled. By then the costs of dissent—ostracism and vilification—were clear, and a majority of members were irrevocably committed to seeing, hearing, and speaking no evil of their leader.

Their initial dereliction wasn't the willingness to forgive Romero's apparent misconduct when it was exposed in 2003 but the decision to label it an innocent mistake. Small lies about minor managerial lapses may seem inconsequential, but they are perhaps more indicative of flawed character than large lies about serious malfeasance: even generally honest people will lie when they must, when the costs of truth telling are high. It takes a congenital liar to evade and deny the truth reflexively, when the costs of acknowledging it are low.

"Come clean, if you purposefully misled them," one ACLU insider recalls advising Romero, who nervously consulted him about the consent agreement controversy, in the summer of 2003. But board members told themselves and each other that there was no need for Romero to admit the truth as long as he knew they suspected it. Executive committee member Rob Remar privately assured me that Romero had been chastened by the controversy over his conduct and had "learned his lesson." Indeed. He apparently learned that he could rely on the president and executive committee to disarm or discredit his critics and cover for his "mistakes," as they repeatedly would. In any case, Romero seemed much more angered than chastened even by tentative efforts to exercise oversight. During a September 2003 conference call with the executive committee, one member futilely suggested presenting a motion to the board that gently faulted Romero and reminded him to provide the executive committee with timely information in the future. Romero responded, offline, but on tape, "Oh, you know, you can kiss my ass." And they did.[6]

II

It's hardly unusual for a group engaged in a common, presumptively noble endeavor to prefer camaraderie to conflict, making a virtue out of a willingness to ignore or trivialize serious managerial failures. But the ACLU board chose this particular path of no resistance when the vices of doing so were particularly clear, during an era of corporate scandal: Enron declared bankruptcy in 2001. Former Tyco CEO Dennis Kozlowski was indicted for tax evasion in 2002. Adelphia Communications filed for bankruptcy in 2002, after the indictment of its former CEO, John Rigas. Former WorldCom CEO Bernie Ebbers was fired in 2002 and indicted in August 2003—the same month that the ACLU executive committee was busy averting an inquiry into the executive director's truthfulness. In response to this wave of scandal, the controversial Sarbanes-Oxley Act (promulgating new accounting standards for public companies) was enacted in 2002, the year before Romero's evasions were first exposed and the ACLU board offered him support, instead of subjecting him to oversight.

But Enron-era scandals involved money—exceedingly large sums of it. The harm caused by corporate wrongdoing was widespread and quantifiable. In the nonprofit world, too, dishonest or otherwise unprincipled behavior is likely to be ignored unless it involves money or, on occasion, sex. Former United Way president William Aramony was forced out after embarrassing publicity about his misuse of funds. Widely publicized financial improprieties also resulted in the resignation of several top officials at the Smithsonian. The American Red Cross, by 2008 under the direction of its seventh president since 2002, has been sharply criticized by government watchdogs for its fundraising practices, notably the tendency to raise much more money than it needs or effectively uses for relief efforts.

Romero had not been caught lying about money, and board members who might have been aroused by financial abuses apparently didn't worry that a relatively secretive executive director of questionable honesty who seemed subject to relatively little oversight might be an untrustworthy steward of the organization's principles, if not its finances. The bottom line for an advocacy group or charity is not supposed to be financial; instead, it is sometimes compelled by principle or its professed moral code to make financial sacrifices, as the Catholic Church may have belatedly learned after focusing on its financial liability for child abuse instead of its moral obligation to protect children. Conversely, when the ACLU defended the rights of neo-Nazis to march in Skokie, Illinois, in 1977, it incurred substantial financial losses (at a time of relative organizational poverty) but preserved its essential commitment to civil liberty. But during the Bush years, the ACLU grew rich, and generally the board seemed less troubled by violations of principle than delighted by increasing prosperity. I doubt that many members ever considered the relevance of widely publicized governance failures by corporate boards to their own roles as fiduciaries. The ACLU board would not or could not seriously entertain the notion that its leaders might be as likely to abuse power as the leaders of multibillion-dollar corporations, absent substantial checks on their behavior.

Yet ACLU leaders had grossly abused power in the past: As the national board eventually acknowledged in 1980, "some ACLU officials" collaborated with the FBI during mid-twentieth-century red scares, informing on ACLU activists, sharing internal documents, and consulting FBI officials about "pending actions or policy discussions."[7] The board had facilitated these abuses, enacting a loyalty oath in 1940 and expelling board member Elizabeth Gurley Flynn for her membership in the Communist Party. So the ACLU's own widely known history offered a lesson in organizational hubris and the temptation to abandon principle during times of stress, in the interests of political viability. But the lesson was ignored. The likelihood, or mere possibility, that the ACLU might yield to the pressures of the war on terror as it had once yielded to the war on communism seems never to have occurred to board members in the post-9/11 era. The ACLU had fallen far in the 1940s and '50s, but that was then.

Naturally, Romero and lay leaders welcomed this laissez-faire attitude toward governance and enlisted expert opinion encouraging it. In the fall of 2003, after our brief battle over the consent-agreement debacle, the leadership engaged a management consultant, Susan Gross, who advised the executive committee (at a November 2003 meeting) that "lay leadership is a mythology," citing another not-for-profit organization that renamed its board an "assembly" and "gave up the conceit that this group was the governance body." She advised that the full ACLU board (as opposed to the executive committee) had virtually no governance responsibilities and no authority to question or evaluate the executive director (whom she seemed to be channeling); board members should focus exclusively on the "performance of the institution"—as if unethical conduct of staff would have no effect on institutional "performance" and would only matter in the unlikely event that it did.[8]

But whether or not abandoning the "conceit" that a board is a governing body is typical or desirable organizational behavior, as Gross suggested, it conflicts with the ACLU's bedrock belief in monitoring and mistrusting authority— the wisdom of which is periodically confirmed by corporate and government abuses. "We should not trust our institutions unless we can be confident that someone is distrusting the officials who run them," ethicist and political theorist Dennis Thompson writes in *Restoring Responsibility*. Reviewing scandals at Enron, the FBI, and the Catholic Church, he notes, "The priests who abused power, the CEOs and CFOs who cooked the books, and the FBI desk officers in Washington—they were all trusted too much by their overseers." Thompson stresses the inaptness of trust in shaping institutional as opposed to individual relationships: "Trust is an interpersonal interaction." The "practical ethics" necessary for guiding institutional life require distrust or "an ethics of oversight" ensuring that we "punish overseers for acts of omission as much as for acts of commission . . . offenses of oversight as much as for the primary offenses over which the oversight is exercised."[9]

Thompson's insights might have been embraced in principle at the ACLU, but the board was unwilling or unable to put them into practice; and a majority of the leadership listened approvingly as Susan Gross offered a contrary vision of institutional ethics: The board and the CEO should have a partnership, she said; but people in the ACLU "talk about the board as a watchdog. A watchdog looks for wrongdoing," she warned "and that's not a partnership." Acknowledging that she had not read the ACLU's bylaws, she criticized their extensiveness, which she considered an indication that the ACLU was "a group of people acting out of mistrust." If only.

That a group bound together by an ideology of mistrust would bow to the demand of its own leadership to "trust us" is a testament to the conflict between reason and solidarity; partisanship demands irrationalism when members are expected not simply to support their team but to suspend judgment of it, even within the confines of the locker room. An ethic of trust at the ACLU that discouraged board members from overseeing the conduct of their leaders was intellectually and ideologically incoherent, but in defining and fulfilling their organizational responsibilities, members seemed increasingly less influenced by reason or principle than by conflict aversion, the need to belong, and faith in the ACLU's immutable goodness.

Exceptionalism is a familiar moral hazard, for individuals as well as the groups they compose, and many of us at the ACLU were guilty of it. While I pointed disapprovingly to the negligence or arrogance of the board in disdaining principles of governance and civil liberty, and presuming the ACLU incorruptible, the leadership and its many supporters accused me of hubris for disdaining the decisions and predilections of the group.

When are we obliged to obey rules, or customs, and when are we justified in breaking them? These are not exactly unfamiliar questions for the ACLU, which grew out of efforts to defend antiwar protesters and draft dodgers during World

War I. The ACLU enshrined the belief that ethics was not simply a matter of following rules, yet it did not advocate anarchy. Rules matter at the ACLU (as its devotion to litigation shows), but the rules that matter most are those that restrain government and prevent arbitrary exercises of power. The ACLU is supposed to focus on making sure that government plays by rules establishing fair and neutral legal processes designed to accommodate dissent and divergent faiths or ideologies.

A commitment to process requires, even assumes, a commitment to honesty, which is why perjury is a serious offense that should trouble civil libertarians. Lying undermines the fair and accurate evaluation of conflicting claims or principles, obviously. How can you assess or adjudicate claims that are based on fiction, not fact? Even white lies can be problematic, not because in telling them you follow your conscience instead of the rules, but because you do so covertly, subverting rules you're pretending to obey: Imagine that you're called for jury duty in a death-penalty case. You have serious moral qualms about capital punishment, but you know that if you acknowledge them, you will be disqualified from jury service. Is justice served if you tell the truth or if you lie? If you consider the automatic disqualification of death-penalty skeptics unjust (as I do), you might feel compelled to tell what you'd fairly characterize as a white lie (and most defense attorneys to whom I've posed this little dilemma agree that lying about your views would be ethically obligatory). But I bet that police officers who lie about the circumstances of illegal searches that turned up concealed weapons or other contraband think that they're telling white lies, too, although most defense attorneys would disagree. I'm not sure how you should respond as a juror asked to rule on a case involving a law you consider unjust (I'm not sure how I'd respond). But I am reasonably confident that in a relatively democratic society or group in which justice is possible, truth is generally a better hedge against injustice than lies.

Questions about the morality of lying are merely academic, however, if you characterize lies as errors or even fibs. Fibs generate little if any moral outrage and their practical effects are barely discernible. Focusing on the evils of fibbing seems merely priggish. Still, the effort to cover up or trivialize lying at least reflects discomfort with it: the ACLU board could not easily excuse lies that were openly acknowledged; honesty was supposed to be among its core values.

But honesty is not an advantage in an intensely competitive, survivor culture, in which people may be expected to lie or otherwise cheat or sabotage their opponents in order to win. In political campaigns, where public welfare, not private aggrandizement, is supposed to be a priority, some candidates successfully exploit this ethic even as they pretend to disdain it. How do they reconcile ruthless solipsism with a professed commitment to community? By convincing voters that the willingness to say, do, or be anything to get elected is a sign of strength, fortitude, and an admirable unwillingness to lose that will be exercised in the interests of the public. "I'm not fighting (or cheating) for me, I'm fighting (or cheating) for you," is the implicit message of their campaigns.

Outside the political sphere, in the arena of reality TV, self-centeredness and an unmitigated commitment to victory are celebrated without apology or pretense: there, self-interest need not be equated with the interests of the collective. Self-restraint in deference to fair play or principle is for losers, along with self-doubt. Everyone is in it to win it—"psyched" and "ready to do whatever it takes." Whether they're vying for a cash prize or a rose or simply their share of airtime, many of the "real" people who populate reality TV are true believers in self-promotion (the putative virtues of which follow from popular nostrums about self-esteem). Fluent in hyperbole, they succeed or strive to succeed partly by aggressively marketing themselves. The spectacle is familiar. On and off camera, we "definitely" inhabit a culture of emphatic affirmation: "absolutely" is the new "yes." If the "real" world of TV is scripted and edited, it still accurately reflects the mixed American marriage of pop psychology and intense competitiveness. The therapeutic mandate to feel good about yourself helps sanctify the drive to prevail over all others. On reality TV, the exhibitionism of participants seems partly to reflect the pride they take in their own strategic unscrupulousness, and the admiration, however grudging, it inspires among viewers.

This was part of the larger culture in which the ACLU story unfolded. Like reality TV stars, ACLU leaders focused single-mindedly on owning the island, in no small part through "image control": public relations campaigns as well as internal cover-ups would prove central to their success. Like political candidates, they convinced the board (and perhaps themselves) that their interests coincided with the interests of the organization—that they were fighting (or cheating) for the ACLU. Lies that served the leadership's self-interests were likely to be rationalized by board members who knew the truth as lies told out of loyalty to the group. Or lying was admired—when cast as "messaging" or clever PR spin. Manipulating the board, persuading it to cover up or overlook their deceitfulness, ACLU leaders appealed to teamwork without actually engaging in it. What was good for them was not, in fact, good for the ACLU.

4

The Political
Shouldn't Be Personal

I

The hesitancy of board leaders to assert their authority over a testy executive director is not atypical in the not-for-profit world, where it's often considered "bad manners for boards to carry out too much oversight," where people tend to be less interested in governance than in supporting and identifying with a cause.[1] But the ACLU board had not been typical and timid about challenging its former executive director, Ira Glasser, with whom it regularly battled. After Anthony Romero took over, it surrendered; board members learned to cheer the executive director when they should have challenged him.

There was no single explanation for this new submissiveness; like most cultural changes, it was overdetermined—partly by Romero's personality and the reactions it elicited, partly by his demographic profile, and perhaps most of all by 9/11 and the unprecedented wealth it generated for the ACLU, along with unprecedented threats to civil liberty: As a May 1, 2001, press release announcing Romero's appointment boasted, he was "the first Latino and openly gay man to head the ACLU." At thirty-five, he also represented a new generation of progressives. A former Ford Foundation executive, he brought a less scrappy, more cautious, corporate perspective to the ACLU, which became increasingly dominant as the organization became increasingly rich in the aftermath of 9/11. Romero skillfully cultivated gazillionaire donors who made seven- and eight-figure gifts and whose patronage effectively replaced board oversight; the ACLU's nouveau wealth gave him nouveau power to reward the loyalty of national and affiliate staff and instill the fear of retaliation in those even suspected of disloyalty. (Discretionary grants from the national office to affiliates greatly increased, and several affiliate executive directors privately acknowledged that they refrained from questioning national practices so as not to jeopardize their funding. National staff reportedly acknowledged to one affiliate that financial support for its civil liberties battles depended on a show of unquestioning loyalty to the ACLU leadership.) But 9/11 was Romero's trump card (although it turned out to be a joker). Criticizing him threatened to destabilize the ACLU in the midst of its campaign to keep America "safe and free," especially when the criticisms exposed the hypocrisies of the safe-and-free campaign. From the leadership's perspective, our criticisms of Romero undermined the ACLU's defense of liberty; from our perspective, the ACLU's defense of liberty was deeply compromised by Romero's conduct and its approval by lay leaders.

The organization devolved ideologically as well as ethically, as it stopped practicing what it preached, perhaps unavoidably. A loss of intellectual honesty isn't easily contained; an advocacy group that manages itself hypocritically is likely to manage its mission hypocritically (and ultimately ineffectively) too. But before turning to the political costs of this decline, it helps to understand the personal dynamics that unleashed the demons of association at the ACLU.

This is how executive committee member and general counsel Susan Herman (recently elected ACLU president) explained her decision not to press Romero for the truth when reviewing his handling of the consent agreement with the New York attorney general (and I paraphrase): "Imagine that you're the mother of a teenager," she posited. "He comes home late, in violation of his curfew, and you demand to know why. He offers a series of excuses that you know to be false. At that point, you have a decision to make: you can either challenge his excuses and continue demanding the truth, or you can accept the excuses, letting him know that you do not want him violating curfew again."[2]

It was a stunningly inapt but telling analogy: Romero was relatively young (then in his late thirties), but he was not a teenage boy; he was a grown-up, who had assumed grown-up responsibilities as head of the nation's leading civil liberties organization. Executive committee members were not his parents. They were fiduciaries, charged with overseeing his efforts in the interests of the organization. But if they had an intellectual understanding of their roles, they didn't act on it. (Commenting privately on their tolerance of Romero's behavior, one board member likened the executive committee to the parents of a teenager with an obvious but unacknowledged substance-abuse problem.) In fact, the majority of committee members, including the president, were at least fifteen years older than Romero; a few were old enough to be his parents. He sometimes acted like a recalcitrant, resentful child in their presence (throwing the occasional tantrum), and he had an apparent habit of establishing faux, filial relationships with his elders, if they were in a position to help him. "I have always greatly admired you—and have regarded you as a surrogate father figure," he stressed in a July 28, 2004, e-mail to Ira Glasser, who had encouraged Romero's bid to succeed him at the helm of the ACLU.

Romero's penchant for personalizing professional relationships may have been a reflex, but it was also an effective strategy, inspiring patronage and protectiveness in people who might otherwise be tempted to reprimand him, fire him, or cut off his funding; in addition, it was a defense against substantive critiques of his policy positions. His July 28 e-mail appealing to Glasser's paternal instincts exemplified his tendency to counter intellectual arguments with emotional outbursts or pleas. Romero's e-mail was a response to this dispute: in his capacity as chair of the Drug Policy Alliance (DPA), Glasser and DPA executive director Ethan Nadelmann had written to the Ford Foundation persuasively (but unsuccessfully) assailing a grant agreement restricting the speech of grantees—an agreement that Romero had quietly helped craft and covertly approved on behalf of the ACLU. (DPA eventually declined a grant when Ford refused to amend or delete its restriction on speech.) Romero reportedly reacted to DPA's appeal to Ford with self-pitying fury, angrily confronting Nadelmann and, in his e-mail exchange with Glasser, complaining that because he had regarded Glasser as a "surrogate father," he had been "hurt so much" by his critique.

Glasser was apparently unmoved. ("None of this is personal. . . . It is an institutional disagreement, not a personal matter between us as individuals," he replied.) But Romero's personal appeals (implicit and explicit) were quite successful at the ACLU board, inviting sympathy and deterring criticism of his policies as well as his conduct. The board's relationship to its executive director changed dramatically with his appointment partly because it was confronted with a very different personality: the intensely competitive Glasser regarded argument as sport and welcomed every challenge to his judgment as another opportunity to win. He was a skilled, aggressive, merciless debater, and some board members felt steamrolled by him; but he addressed the merits of issues and appreciated a good fight, which a sufficient number of board members gave him. His combativeness, his comfort in the arena, implicitly invited the board to spar with him—and it did, to the benefit of the organization. Romero, who lacked an impressive command of the issues, seemed ill at ease arguing and resentful of challenges to his positions. Treating them as personal attacks, he responded not with argument but with emotional hostility—hurt, anger, or defensiveness—that deterred board oversight, more than Glasser's combativeness ever could.

Romero's tendency to personalize policy disputes surfaced fairly early in his tenure, during a debate about a proposed affirmative action policy for the national board (which was eventually adopted). I opposed the policy; in a paroxysm of political correctness, it established affirmative action categories and goals for women, disabled people, gay, lesbian, bisexual, and transgendered people (GLBTs), as well as various racial and ethnic minorities. Only healthy, heterosexual white males would be precluded from claiming membership in an affirmative action class to gain an advantage in securing a position on the ACLU board, but they could look forward to aging and developing a disability.

Discussions of this policy (which filled many hours and I've forgotten how many meetings) were sometimes tense and marked by at least a little self-censorship: if you feared being labeled insensitive or insufficiently committed to equality, you criticized affirmative action policies euphemistically or not at all. Sometimes the discussions were emotional: one board member offered tearful testimony about the comfort he derived from the presence of colleagues who were members of his category. But Oprah moments like this were few; discussions of the affirmative action policy (like most board discussions) tended to be short on melodrama and exceedingly long on debate.

Then, in a January 2003 meeting, a little over a year into Romero's tenure (and before the emergence of disputes about his conduct), I spoke in opposition to affirmative action "goals" that effectively functioned like quotas. In referring to "quotas" I offended Romero, a beneficiary of affirmative action, who subsequently intervened to caution us against using the language of affirmative action's "enemies." He didn't single me out, but I soon rose again to speak, acknowledging that I had been the miscreant who had uttered the word "quota," and uttering it again when I resumed arguing against the quota-like goals in our policy. Romero exploded, calling me out and yelling that if I wanted to use the word "quota," I should "join my friends at the Ashcroft Justice Department."

His outburst was met with an audible gasp (even from people who didn't like me), and during a break, several board members tried to reason with him, explaining that I had not been arguing against affirmative action in general or suggesting that all affirmative action plans involved quotas (that line of argument might have been verboten). But Romero remained angry, exclaiming that after he was named ACLU executive director, a major donor told him dismissively that he owed his job to his ethnicity. At the time I believed this little tale. (Knowing him as I do now, I suspect that it was fabricated.) I felt sorry for him (he had embarrassed himself) and attributed his momentary loss of reason to an understandable sensitivity about affirmative action. I approached him later to make peace, and he offered me a piece of chocolate, which I accepted as the apology he couldn't quite bring himself to voice.

But my sympathy for Romero has long since dissipated; recapping this episode, I recognize his characteristic, perhaps instinctive resort to anger and self-pity to repel criticism and counter an argument for which he lacks a rebuttal. With his story of being dissed by an ACLU donor as an affirmative action hire, he manipulated us into comforting him for the insult and assuring him how much we appreciated his achievements, instead of criticizing his rather childish disruption of a board debate. Emotional manipulation was Romero's forte, although he would often use anger not to evoke pity but to intimidate board members who might disapprove of his conduct but were timid in exercising oversight or anxious about avoiding emotional conflicts; tantrums seemed to help Romero consolidate power. Watching the interactions at executive committee meetings (which I occasionally attended) was like watching a child control his parents with the threat of bad behavior.

Perhaps board members would have expressed impatience with Romero's immaturity instead of solicitude for his youth (even as he was pushing forty) had they not been wary of criticizing the ACLU's first gay, Latino leader. Charges of misconduct, no matter how well documented, were periodically condemned as racist or homophobic. "Why don't you come out and admit that your problems lie almost solely with the choice of a bold Gay Puerto Rican American as our ED," one board member demanded, in a public e-mail to me and Michael Meyers in December 2004. I have always doubted that many people took this attack seriously, although I don't recall anyone refuting it, and crying bigotry is usually an effective rhetorical gambit. But it was not just fear of appearing bigoted or insensitive that helped deter people from criticizing Romero; it was also uncertainty about the standards to apply to his behavior. Some suggested (usually in private) that we should consider his cultural background in making allowances for him, as if gay Hispanic people were more prone to lie than Anglo heterosexuals. I don't believe the insult was intended, or even recognized. I attributed the patronizing concern about Romero's "culture" (usually referring to his ethnicity, not his sexual orientation) to the self-conscious diffidence of white liberals charged with overseeing their "bold Gay Puerto Rican American" executive director.

This preoccupation with racism was also rooted in the circumstances of Romero's appointment in 2001: it had opened a racial divide on the board's executive committee, which had doubled as the search committee for Glasser's successor. (I was among the board members who foolishly approved this arrangement, which ensured that the executive committee would be deeply invested in defending the new executive director against board critics, regardless of his performance.) Romero was one of two finalists for the ACLU job; the other was an African American male whose candidacy was strongly supported by the only two African Americans on the executive/search committee, Michael Meyers and James Ferguson. Both had been board leaders for years: Meyers, executive director of the New York Civil Rights Coalition, armed with an encyclopedic knowledge of board policies and procedures and a sharp intelligence, is a difficult, provocative personality. (He makes me look like

Mary Tyler Moore.) "You're a pain in the ass," I once told him. "But I'm a necessary pain in the ass," he rightly replied. Ferguson, a prominent North Carolina attorney and one of the most popular and respected ACLU leaders, was always dignified, judicious, and conciliatory.

They appealed the committee's decision to the full board, unsuccessfully, and were graceful in defeat, ultimately supporting the majority's choice. But the effects of their initial opposition to Romero lingered; both Meyers and Ferguson eventually became quite critical of his conduct, and their criticisms (along with the criticisms of board members who did not oppose him initially) were frequently attributed to presumed resentment over his selection. Meyers was defeated for reelection to the board in 2005; Ferguson resigned in 2006, posting a statement at savetheaclu.org that stressed "the persistent refusal of leadership to recognize and accept that there is a problem within, even as our external program retains a facade of respectability. . . . There have been far too many instances over a prolonged period of time where national lay leadership has shown its unwillingness to address forthrightly serious errors in the conduct and judgment of the Executive Director to the detriment of the Union. . . . These errors [were] repeated over and over again, and followed by transparent attempts to cover them up and deny their seriousness."

The cover-ups and denials that Ferguson cited began when the board met in October 2003 to discuss the controversy over the 2002 consent agreement with the attorney general in an unrecorded, two-hour closed session, attended and dominated by outside counsel hired by Romero. Shortly before the meeting, we had been buried in documents with varying degrees of relevance to questions about Romero's conduct and the ACLU's potential liability. At the conclusion of a presentation by counsel and the board leadership, we embarked on an unusual exercise in peer pressure, proposed by the executive committee. Instead of conducting our customary, unstructured debate, during which board members raise their hands to speak when they have something to say, engaging each other in argument, the board president called on every board member in turn, allowing each a minute or two to speak. Their statements were predictable and probably preordained: board members had been successfully lobbied by the executive committee, which had quickly closed ranks around the executive director; while a significant minority (about twenty people) remained unconvinced of his probity and confidentially expressed strong disapproval of his conduct, only a few were willing to criticize Romero openly, as one by one, people stood and pledged their support to him. A smarter person than I would have realized then that with this ritual exchange of vows, the group was committing itself irrevocably to forgiving and forgetting Romero's "mistakes." Squelching self-criticism, it was embracing self-congratulation.

As majority support for the leadership hardened, so did our small minority's opposition to it, provoked by what we considered its fiduciary failures and, most of all, its fundamental dishonesty. A few months later, in January 2004, board member Muriel Morisey, who teaches ethics at Temple Law School, filed a grievance with the New York bar against outside counsel hired by Romero to defend his handling of the consent agreement. (Morisey alleged that counsel had offered unethical advice, partly intended to obscure Romero's violation of the agreement. She eventually decided not to pursue the grievance because the advice had not been recorded.) My purpose here is not to debate the merits of Morisey's complaint but to examine the role of the ACLU executive committee in prompting her to take the extraordinary step of filing it.[3]

Morisey first outlined her concerns privately in an October 20, 2003, e-mail to executive committee member Ron Chen. She repeated them in a subsequent November 21, 2003, e-mail to the entire executive committee, requesting additional information about payments to outside counsel and the fine paid to settle the attorney general's privacy complaint, as well as a legal analysis of her ethical question. Then she waited vainly for a response; the executive committee ignored her, failing even to acknowledge receipt of her e-mail, although (as she learned later) the committee did quietly consult the lawyers who were named in her complaint. Receiving no response or acknowledgment for two months, Morisey struggled to balance what she considered her ethical obligations as a lawyer with her role as a board member and her regard for the institution. In the end, Morisey said, she asked herself how she would want her students to resolve a similar ethical dilemma. She filed her grievance on January 20, 2004.

Morisey was the first board member (but would not be the last) to air her concerns about misconduct externally, and her decision to do so should have served as a warning to ACLU leadership: when a group turns its back on members who question its integrity or fundamental competence (whether the group is devoted to manufacturing widgets or protecting civil liberties), when internal processes for hearing and resolving ethical or managerial concerns are corrupted, dissenters seek external remedies. Morisey had a long history of service to the ACLU, both as staff and board member; her institutional loyalty was strong, and she would not have filed a formal grievance if the executive committee had responded to her concerns and considered them fairly and honestly, whether or not anyone ended up agreeing with her. No sane person aspires to whistle-blowing; the costs are certain —loss of a job or career, or status, at least, not to mention enormous aggravation—while the rewards, for the individual and the organization, are highly speculative. For Morisey, appealing to an external authority was her last resort, and not surprisingly, it failed.

Whistle-blowing is one signal that associational virtues have devolved into vice, solidifying resistance to reform. By the time a group has committed itself to ignoring or reflexively discrediting internal critics, whistle-blowing is apt to exacerbate the problems that it reflects—tribalism, conformity, obedience to authority, and the suppression of dissent. Naturally, Morisey's decision to lodge a formal complaint against the ACLU's outside counsel enraged many board members, tightening their ranks, turning impatience with dissent into intolerance for it. Naturally, she was condemned by the president and members of the executive committee, several of whom denied any responsibility for ignoring her and (according to Morisey) claimed that they had not discussed or even been aware of her concerns when they met in November 2003. That claim was false, as a transcript of the November meeting showed. Naturally, few board members seemed to care, and practically none offered support for Morisey in public.

II

Privately, some members who supported the leadership acknowledged the apparent disingenuousness of its defenses, but they continued insisting that by covering up bad behavior and protecting the ACLU from bad publicity, they were protecting civil liberty. They also rationalized the cover-ups as acts of forgiveness offered to an erring executive director beset by mean, morally intransigent critics, or "egocentric assholes," a description offered by one executive committee member in an e-mail to the board and seconded by many. People who were uncomfortable tolerating or promoting stories they knew were untrue could still tell themselves and each other that they were acting, in part, out of kindness. Personalizing its relationship with the executive director, acting on the pretense that the ACLU was a family, the board treated Romero like a relative it hadn't chosen and couldn't disown. Nurturance effectively replaced oversight as the board's primary fiduciary responsibility; accountability, much less whistle-blowing, seemed practically akin to child abuse.

We are all family in an apolitical, therapeutic culture that focuses narrowly on personal development and interpersonal relations. Organizations and institutions are virtual or surrogate families, as is the workplace, in a popular sitcom trope that dates back at least to the 1970s. So although the familial metaphor was powerful at the ACLU partly because of the particular personalities at play, it was hardly unique to the ACLU; it also reflected national cultural trends.

America's innumerable support groups constitute a primary model of associational life, for religionists and secularists, liberals and conservatives alike. In her study of group membership and moral development, political theorist Nancy Rosenblum observes that small support groups devoted to personal development (religious, spiritual, or secular) involve an estimated 75 million Americans. While acknowledging their personalized focus on "caring" and "self-transformation," instead of on civic engagement, Rosenblum surmises that these groups may, nonetheless, instill "democratic dispositions" in their members, like organizational skills and the ability to engage with fellow citizens or even speak up (in the therapeutic vernacular, "testify") about perceived wrongs.[4]

If the experiences as well as ideologies of support groups cultivate social or civic habits in their participants, as Rosenblum sensibly suggests, they probably cultivate associational habits too. While we can't quantify the influence of the support group dynamic on relationships and roles within nontherapeutic groups, we would be foolish to discount it. At the Massachusetts ACLU, for example, uncontested board elections are justified by solicitude for the "feelings" of losing candidates (even if they primarily benefit insiders intent on retaining control). A pervasive preoccupation with civility in associational and institutional life, at the expense of vigorous debate (even the ACLU has considered civility codes), partly reflects pop therapeutic notions of a supportive, "caring" community. Howard County, Maryland, for example, is one of several localities sponsoring a "civility project," the *Wall Street Journal* tartly reported in April 2008. Based on a book by a Johns Hopkins University "professor of civility," it's supposed to build connections between residents and inspire goodness in them—assuming they internalize rules like "Be Agreeable" and "Accept and Give Praise."[5]

This is a stereotypically feminine ethic, and graduates of women's groups and institutions may recognize its unreliability. Requiring graciousness and agreeability drives disagreeability underground, where it festers rather treacherously. On the rare occasion when criticism is openly expressed in violation of the agreeability mandate, it's punished disproportionately. The demand for praise exaggerates the harm of criticism, encouraging irrational responses to it. The petty cruelties encouraged by a presumptively feminine preoccupation with niceness are illustrated by this spat within the U.S. women's soccer team, reported in the *New York Times*: Goalkeeper Hope Solo was shunned by the team because she sharply protested a decision to take her out of a 2007 World Cup semifinals match (which the United States then lost 4–0) and implicitly criticized the player who replaced her (the highly regarded Brianna Scurry). Solo made these disagreeable remarks while mourning the sudden death of her father, as well as the loss of the match. But even her grief was apparently no excuse: "She was ostracized by [the coach] and by her teammates, prohibited from joining them for the third-place game against Norway, from eating team meals, even from traveling home on the same flight. The telephone calls that used to come on days off—let's go shopping, let's go to the beach—no longer come."[6]

This sorry little episode reflects a rather dysfunctional notion of teamwork, and it dramatizes the dangers of personalizing professional relationships. Whether or not team members shop together, they ought to be able to compete together. As Hope Solo commented to the *New York Times,* "We don't have to be friends, we don't even have to like each other, but you will respect one another on the field. You just play."

Exactly. Protesting an ethic of caring may seem rather churlish, but it tends to be an ethic of convenience, as the women's soccer team demonstrated; that is, practitioners of it generally extend support to whomever they like or approve, withholding it from whomever they dislike or view with trepidation. And why shouldn't they? How couldn't they? Caring is not mere courtesy, and it's not reasonable or realistic to expect people to be more than courteous to those for whom they bear no genuine good will (apart from family members or others to whom they have professional obligations). Most of us are probably incapable of caring without discrimination or at least a hope of mutuality; pretending otherwise doesn't make us nice; it makes us hypocritical. (At the ACLU, the same board member who regularly mocked me and other dissenters, suggesting that we "fuck off and die" and referring to me as a "fucked out boozy bitch," also declared, with no apparent self-awareness, that we should not "hold board members up for ridicule"; he offered this plea for civility in the course of defending a proposal to bar board members from criticizing the ACLU.) Pretending to be nicer and more caring than we are capable or even desirous of being also makes us untrustworthy. Outside the ambit of actual families and close friends, fairness and honesty are much more reliable guarantees of virtue than "niceness" can ever be. Fairness is what we owe and can deliver to acquaintances or colleagues for whom we really don't care; honesty is what enables us to trust them and work together productively. In associations and institutions that put a premium on niceness or even civility, you should probably never stop looking over your shoulder.

The virtues we seek in personal relationships may function as vices in organizational life, ethicist Dennis Thompson stresses in *Restoring Responsibility*: "The tendency to let individual ethics dominate institutional ethics—what may be called the privatization of ethics—is a mistake. . . . Many of the moral virtues that we praise in individual relations can produce bad consequences in organizational life. Loyalty to family and friends is a quality we admire in private life, but it is a common source of favoritism and corruption in public life." It denigrates whistle-blowing as informing, Thompson notes, eliding the differences between them: "Whistleblowers sooner or later make their protests public (and are often penalized rather than rewarded)," and their actions serve the interests of the collective, "whatever their motives." Personal dislike for "the kind of person who is capable of blowing the whistle" should not "determine how we act in corporate life and how we design institutions."[7] Or, as goalkeeper Hope Solo suggested, you don't have to like your teammates to respect and work productively with them, appreciating their contributions to a common endeavor.

Labeling whistle-blowers rats obviously makes corruption difficult to uncover, much less remedy. Elia Kazan's classic 1954 film about union corruption, *On the Waterfront,* persuasively advocates choosing legal or communal obligations over personal loyalties, defending informing as bearing witness, at least when the witness is a magnetic, young Marlon Brando testifying about the murder of an innocent. When the witness is a middle-aged Elia Kazan, naming names before the House Un-American Activities Committee in 1952, the defense is a bit less compelling, even if you equate the perceived threat of communist subversion in the '50s with homicidal union thuggery: Kazan was protecting his career, acting out of self-interest, not risking his life to protect others.

There's no categorical answer to the question of whether personal or associational obligations should prevail when they conflict; moral dilemmas are resolved with reference to principle but shaped by particular matters of facts. But when obligations to individuals and collectives are conflated, ethical conflicts between them aren't even recognized, much less resolved, and ethical problems abound. "Loyalty calls for different inclinations and judgments in organizational life from those it requires in personal relations. So does compassion," as Thompson observes.[8] CEOs sometimes have an ethical obligation to fire people with whom they sympathize. So do boards. It's difficult to argue against mercy, especially in personal relationships. But in organizational or political life, mercy is often a lesser virtue than justice.

The elevation of mercy or personal loyalty over institutional obligations often presages complicity in wrongdoing. Groups that tolerate the misconduct of their leaders out of loyalty or compassion, at first, are likely to end up covering for it out of self-interest (which will invariably be equated with the organization's interest). At the ACLU, board members who forgave the executive director without ever holding him accountable were soon forgiving themselves as well. Once acknowledged, misconduct could not justifiably be ignored; conversely, once ignored, it could not be acknowledged as misconduct. This charade implicitly presumed that Romero's failings, and the board's, were personal and had no significant institutional consequences requiring institutional action. Having personalized organizational relationships, the board ended up personalizing organizational conduct too, developing the inappropriately narrow view of moral responsibility that Thompson identifies as another consequence of personalizing organizational ethics. In private life, "this limited view of moral responsibility makes some sense. . . . It is not your fault if other people lie." But in an organization, this view "suggests an ethic of merely keeping your own hands clean."[9]

The public interest is not exactly a priority in these private, personalized environments, and neither are the interests of the group. Focusing on the personality and welfare of their leader, group members easily lose sight of where his interests end and the interests of the group begin. Denying their obligation to protest the unethical actions of others, members legitimize conspiracies of silence. Eventually, no one is responsible for preventing and remedying organizational misconduct; eventually, few can even recognize it.

5

Facts Don't Matter

I

The story of the ACLU's degeneration is not simple or sensational. Our litany of charges against the leadership bored as well as angered many people and was easily trivialized as "inside baseball" (although "inside baseball" is the game board members are expected to play). While a small minority of us considered recurring ethical lapses symptomatic of a steady ethical decline, however unimportant they seemed individually, the majority treated them as arcane disputes about mere technicalities.

Criticizing the leadership and proving our allegations of its habitual dishonesty confronted us with a formidable strategic challenge: in order to substantiate claims of misconduct, you have to present a detailed, factual case; but the more details you present, the less likely that people will take the time to consider them. The more we explained and documented, the more we irritated people; the longer and denser our e-mails and memos, the less chance that they would even be read. That practically all of the claims and counterclaims by both sides could be proved or disproved by resort to the factual record was essentially irrelevant. Facts may be stubborn things, but they can still be rendered moot, invisible in a fog of falsehoods. We were easily outmaneuvered by ACLU leaders, who could simply deny the truth of our assertions, attack our motives and institutional loyalty, and transform a dispute about objective, verifiable facts into a convoluted "we said, they said" spat.

There was, then, no need to ferret out the facts: distinguishing truth from lies became a simple matter of distinguishing the good guys from the bad. Predictably, most board members fell in line behind the leadership, assuming its goodness and the truth of its claims and securing their place in the group, instead of joining a handful of aggravating outliers.

It may seem unlikely that a group of civil libertarians would allow themselves to be so easily herded and so readily conform in order to belong, but despite their theoretical commitment to protecting dissent, civil libertarians are mere human beings, apt to retain the usual susceptibilities to peer pressure and the usual needs to be liked and respected by the group with which they choose to identify. (People may feel honored by the dislike of groups they disdain but shamed by the dislike of groups they admire.) The social pressures on a board are like the social pressures in high school, college, and other affinity groups, which is partly why the familiar characterization of whistle-blowers as maladjusted malcontents is sometimes accurate (even when their claims are true). Well-adjusted board members who are liked, respected, and elevated to leadership positions are probably the least likely to engage in whistle-blowing: they have the most to lose, and temperamentally, they tend to be more collegial than contrarian anyway. They didn't achieve prominence in their group by alienating colleagues. Never mind whistle-blowing —airing complaints externally—many hesitate to dissent internally.

Boardroom pressure to conform even affects confident, securely high-status people who know better: Warren Buffet has "ruefully" acknowledged that as an independent director of many public companies, he has fallen prey to the "boardroom atmosphere. . . . Too often I was silent when management made proposals that I judged to be counter to the interests of shareholders. In those cases, collegiality trumped independence," Buffet wrote in 2002, lamenting common failures of corporate governance.[1] "I'm always amazed at how common groupthink is in corporate boardrooms," Jeffrey Sonnenfeld writes. "Directors are, almost without exception, intelligent, accomplished, and comfortable with power. But if you put them into a group that discourages dissent, they nearly always start to conform."[2]

II

Conformity is especially alluring, and dissent seems unduly disruptive, when the group is apparently thriving. ACLU bank accounts and membership rolls swelled in the wake of 9/11, along with the satisfactions of feeling under siege. The more money the organization acquired, the more money it had to lose, the more it focused on protecting and extending its holdings; the board seemed dazzled by dollars, however acquired.

A new devotion to fundraising took hold at the ACLU; it was exemplified by a program involving extensive, relatively secret data mining of donors and members: "The American Civil Liberties Union is using sophisticated technology to collect a wide variety of information about its members and donors in a fund-raising effort that has ignited a bitter debate over its leaders' commitment to privacy rights," a front-page *New York Times* story by Stephanie Strom revealed on December 18, 2004. "Some board members say the extensive data collection makes a mockery of the organization's frequent criticism of banks, corporations and government agencies for their practice of accumulating data on people for marketing and other purposes." Moreover, the *Times* reported, the New York attorney general was conducting an inquiry into whether the group had violated its promises to protect the privacy of donors and members.[3]

Board members generally reacted to these questions about donor privacy with defensiveness or complacency:

major donors often expect to be the subject of research and modest donors often don't object to it (although many are probably unaware of its scope). Characterizing the ACLU's donor research as noncontroversial ("Everybody does it," they said), the leadership and its supporters lambasted the *Times* for the front-page placement of this "nonstory" and excoriated its presumed sources, Michael Meyers and me. "I am furious that I have to wake up and read about it in the newspaper," one board member declared in an e-mail to the board, denouncing this "leak" to the press, as a "home run for the enemies of civil liberties." Directing all his fury at the leakers, he seemed unaware that if Romero had told the board about the new fundraising program, members would not have learned about it from the *New York Times*.

Still, releasing this information to the press instead of the board was at least arguably unfair and understandably angered many board members. It was also arguably justified, given the prevailing tendency to ignore or cover for the executive director's lapses. Staff had reportedly been warned not to reveal the existence of the data-mining initiative to board members, but given the board's passivity, the secrecy surrounding the program may have been quite unnecessary.

The reaction to the *Times* story by national and affiliate board and staff members demonstrated the failures of oversight that prompted the leak to the press. (It did not come from me, but I did not disapprove of it.) Exposure of the data-mining program was treated as another public relations crisis and resulted in another furious round of questionable and sometimes contradictory claims and counterclaims by the leadership, along with accusations that the *Times* report was false and misleading (although, as far as I know, the ACLU did not request corrections and the *Times* did not revise its account). In a set of January 21, 2005, talking points, the ACLU press office declared that the board had been informed of the new data-mining program in an April 2004 budget memo, months before the *Times* story appeared. But that claim was unsupported by the record and undermined by the outrage of board members who wondered why they learned about the program from the press. (The lengthy April 2004 memo included a very brief, general reference to donor research and no substantive description of it.) The insistence that board members knew about the data mining was also flatly contradicted by executive committee member Rob Remar's public avowal of ignorance. In her December 2004 story, *Times* reporter Stephanie Strom cited Remar's assertion that he had only learned a few days earlier (not many months earlier, as the press office claimed) that the ACLU was "using an outside company to collect data or that collection had expanded from major donors to those who contribute as little as $2."[4]

The defense of the data-mining program itself was equally misleading. It rested on the implausible claim that the ACLU's donor-research efforts had not changed significantly in years (some might accuse Romero of negligence if that claim were true) and the repeated reminder that the ACLU collected only publicly available information. But as aging privacy advocates and savvy teenagers know, the scope of easily accessible, public data about us has expanded dramatically in the past decade and includes information that many would consider private. In fact, ACLU policy on data collection laments the covert aggregation of "sensitive personal information" by "powerful modern computer systems" and delineates stringent privacy standards, including informed-consent requirements, for government collection and storage of information about us. After the controversy over the ACLU's data mining arose, the board voted to apply these standards to private, for-profit enterprises engaged in data collection, but not voluntary associations, like the ACLU.[5]

Today, nearly four years after this program was exposed, board members and donors still have relatively little hard information about it. Questions about precisely what methods the ACLU was using to collect what data, who was allowed to access it, and how it was being secured remained unanswered even after a committee on donor research reported briefly to the board in October 2007, over two years after its formation. Finally, in January 2008, a smart, well-informed, previously well-behaved board member voiced strong concerns about the donor-research program (and the ACLU's decision to exempt itself from privacy standards it sought to impose on others) in a detailed memo that he circulated to the entire national board, right before retiring from it. His timing was, perhaps, not coincidental: he would not have to risk ostracism or electoral defeat by pressing his points. They were swatted aside disingenuously (as he might have predicted) and eventually referred back to a committee, on which he sat, instead of being discussed by the full board as he had requested. Controversy was avoided, to the probable relief of those who preferred resting on general assurances from the committee on donor research that the ACLU's program complied with "best practices" governing data collection and retention, that it was "sound, appropriate, and consistent with ACLU policies and principles."

The failure to investigate and question this controversial program typified a collective aversion to oversight that had inevitably hardened as the board closed ranks against dissenters. Having quashed dissent that raised questions about the ACLU's integrity, members could only exercise or pretend to exercise oversight when none was really necessary. Questioning, much less criticizing, the judgment or conduct of staff and lay leaders was considered a serious breach of decorum; it was as if the board had tacitly adopted a de facto civility code requiring the suppression of ethical concerns and inconvenient facts: exposure of the ACLU's donor-research practices sparked a movement to oust Michael Meyers and me.

Less than two weeks after the *Times* reported on the ACLU's data-mining program, Nadine Strossen reported that the executive committee would discuss unseating us at its upcoming January 2005 meeting. In a December 29, 2004, e-mail to the board, she attached a letter she had just received from Cathy Travis, president of the Oregon ACLU affiliate, asking the national board to discuss suspending or impeaching us for talking to the press. Travis did not accuse us of leaking confidential information; instead she stated that we had "allowed [our]selves to be interviewed for attribution and appear to have made misleading statements to a reporter regarding ACLU policy and internal processes." What "misleading statements"? Travis didn't specify; she simply recommended that the board delay considering the merits of our concerns about the data-mining initiative until after it decided whether to punish us for airing them.

In any other organization, on any other board, a member who criticized an organizational initiative in the press might be subject to a reprimand, if not removal, but the ACLU expressly guarantees the right of board members to express opinions publicly "on whatever topics they wish to discuss," whether or not they are in agreement with the ACLU. A free speech policy, adopted thirty years ago, stresses that "as an organization . . . dedicated to protecting freedom of expression from government interference, the ACLU is particularly sensitive to the need to guard the free speech rights of members of its own governing board, staff and other lay leaders against unwarranted interference by the institution itself."[6] With this policy and ACLU values in mind, Strossen could have discouraged the effort to punish us; instead, she distributed Travis's letter to the board immediately upon receiving it and scheduled an executive committee discussion of the proposal to suspend or remove us.

The impeachment movement was abruptly terminated only a few weeks later when *New York Times* reporter Stephanie Strom began inquiring about it. (I had no compunction about talking to a reporter about a movement to impeach me for talking to a reporter.) The president and executive committee quickly disavowed any interest in disciplining us; in an e-mail to the *Times*, Strossen falsely stated that "to the best of [her] knowledge, no current board member supports implementing any such proceedings." In fact, only a day or two before receiving an inquiry from the *Times*, while preparing for a discussion of proceedings against us, Strossen had shared with the executive committee an e-mail from a current board member citing strong majority support for our suspension or impeachment.

Board members who were sympathetic to the impeachment movement and knew that Strossen had facilitated it seemed content with her disingenuous disclaimers to the press. Board members who knew they had not been told about the data-mining program seemed content to rely on official claims that they had known about it all along, just as they relied on the pretense that data collection by voluntary associations was not comparable to data collection by government and private enterprises. Acknowledging that the executive director, president, or press office spread misinformation, or that the ACLU was quietly engaging in data mining at a time when civil libertarians were protesting its use by the Bush administration, would perhaps have generated more cognitive dissonance for board members than any contradiction between what they knew and what they were told. Group solidarity demanded and depended on acceptance of official responses to embarrassing disclosures, regardless of their comportment with known facts.

III

This was not simply a case of biases and expectations shaping perceptions, any more than it was simply a case of inattention. While some members seemed to see and hear only what conformed to their preconceptions about the ACLU and its leaders and some may have taken care to know only what they were told, those who paid any attention had to reconcile glaring contradictions—like their outrage at learning about an ACLU initiative from a newspaper story and their practically simultaneous agreement that the story was old news. I imagine that some justified statements they knew not to be true as white lies. Or maybe they decided that the facts were misleading and their fictions, or fibs, reflective of a deeper truth, as if they were collaborating on a novel instead of overseeing an organization. And some may have convinced themselves that the leadership's version of events was more reliable than their own recollections of them.

Seeing is not believing, or even perceiving, a famous experiment on opinion and social pressure by Solomon Asch demonstrated over fifty years ago: Seven to nine college students are assembled for an experiment in "visual judgment." Only one student is the actual subject; the others are shills working with the experimenter. He shows the group a vertical line drawn on one card and asks members to match it in length with one of three vertical lines shown drawn on another card. The correct answer is obvious, and almost all subjects provide it when they are tested individually. When they're tested in the group, their willingness or ability to answer correctly varies according to the group consensus. Asch put his subjects through a series of tests, varying the discrepancies in lengths of the lines and the group dynamics; about three-quarters of the subjects gave the wrong answer preferred by their groups at least once; on average a little over a third of the subjects echoed the majority's obviously wrong judgment.[7] Asch was surprised and troubled by these results: "That we have found the tendency to conformity in our society so strong that reasonably intelligent and well-meaning young people are willing to call white black is a matter of concern," he observed judiciously.[8]

People who "call white black" in deference to the majority are not, however, necessarily willing or able to acknowledge that they're doing so: "All the yielding subjects underestimated the frequency with which they conformed," Asch noted. You might take some comfort in this suggestion that people don't like admitting how much they conform, even to themselves. But stigmatizing conformity may have little deterrent effect; in the boardroom (and probably in other groups) conformity thrives under an assumed name—collegiality. I'm not suggesting that collegial impulses are necessarily conformist; I'm simply pointing out that conformist impulses are often called collegial.

Conformity is a particularly sensitive subject at the ACLU,

where people pride themselves on their rebelliousness and rejection of majority rule. But naturally, many still find strength in numbers; they stand against majorities outside the ACLU partly because they enjoy the company of a majority within it. They dissent en masse from external majorities and avoid isolation by deferring en masse to the internal ACLU majority, which, in turn, now defers unthinkingly to the ACLU leadership. Personalizing their relationship with the executive director, offering him effusive praise—whether to placate him and counter criticism, suppress conflict, avoid ostracism, or out of a sincere belief in his capabilities—board members inevitability exaggerated his importance to their collective endeavor and, in doing so, expanded his power and entrenched their obedience. The ACLU board seemed to fear the possibility of firing Romero (raised by his defenders early on to deter inquiries into his conduct) almost as much as the unpleasantness of it. When his "mistakes" were first exposed, he had served as executive director for merely two years; the ACLU was about eighty years old, but the board reacted as if the organization would not survive without him.

Instead, it suffered with him. When reasoned admiration of a leader inflates to exaltation, he's apt to lead the organization and its members off a cliff—not always metaphorically, as mass suicides of religious cults attest. The tragedies of Heaven's Gate, the Branch Davidians, or the People's Temple in Jonestown may not have much to teach us about banal organizational decline, but they do illustrate the potentially limitless power of malevolent, unaccountable leaders to define reality for their followers. It's a great leap from successfully exhorting members of a cult to drink poisoned punch and persuading members of an organization to support unethical practices and believe obvious lies in the interests of solidarity, but it is a leap along the same continuum, from one end to the other. Wondering at the ease with which ACLU board members were willing to "call white black," a few of us would regularly sigh and say, "They've drunk the Kool-Aid."

———

Overbearing, self-aggrandizing leaders who demand obedience are not uncommon in American corporate life, Howard F. Stein observes, in the *Journal of Organizational Psychodynamics*. When people or groups feel besieged (as they do today by threats to both security and liberty), "leaders appeal to an us/them polarization, demand unquestioning loyalty, and quash all internal dissent. . . . All opposing views are rejected and doubt is eliminated. . . . Reality testing capacity is impaired."[9] Indeed.

Whether glorifying the leader is cause or effect of glorifying the group he embodies, it elevates maintaining the group's idealized image over confronting the reality of its performance, the degradation of which group members may be the last to perceive. The organizational ideal "can never be attained" (reality is always imperfect) so "organizations often attempt to generate a way of preserving the illusion of [it]," organizational behaviorist Howard S. Schwartz writes. "The attempt to manage the organization by imposing this illusion is . . . 'organizational totalitarianism.' . . . [It] places falsehood right at the core of organizational functioning and therefore cannot help but lead to a loss of rationality." The result is "organizational decay," evidenced most obviously by "the commitment to bad decisions," which tends to be self-perpetuating: the tendency to justify decisions "escalates" commitment to them and the ideas they represent. "Core organizational process becomes the dramatization of the organization and its high officials as ideal [and] the elevation of individuals for promotion and even for continued inclusion comes to be made on the basis of how much they contribute to this dramatization."[10] In other words, the organization dedicates itself to maintaining its image at the cost of its performance, like a cosmetic-surgery junkie who smokes two packs a day.

Schwartz's descriptions of effectively delusional, decaying, or "totalitarian" organizations are strikingly evocative of the ACLU (or so they seem to some disenchanted insiders). As former national board member James Ferguson stressed, the ACLU's program retained merely a "facade of respectability" (what Schwartz might call the "dramatization of the organization"), which board and staff members were rewarded for maintaining and punished for questioning. A series of "transparent" cover-ups demonstrated the "persistent refusal of leadership to recognize . . . a problem within," and in their "zeal" to shield the executive director from criticism of his "repeated transgressions," the board exposed the organization to eventual ideological "collapse."[11]

Do these fears for the ACLU seem outlandish? The suggestion that apparently rational, relatively intelligent individuals readily believe and perpetuate transparent organizational illusions may seem hyperbolic, but it's confirmed by repeated public and private organizational debacles. Schwartz's case studies of NASA and General Motors (which I won't repeat but recommend) demonstrate the expansive capacity for self-deception of people immersed in systems predicated on deceptive images of perfection that repel all suggestions of failure. When Ralph Nader exposed the Corvair's safety hazards in 1965, Schwartz notes, GM "hired private detectives to find ways to discredit him. . . . He had to be a bad person: he had attacked GM, hadn't he?"[12] NASA was supposed to be virtually infallible, and belief in its own infallibility engendered and obscured its decline. "When reality intruded upon NASA's idealization of itself, it appears that NASA suppressed reality," notably the fact that shuttle flights prior to the *Challenger* disaster "were not successes. Many of them were near catastrophes and had been so for a long time."[13]

The catastrophic power of ideals that deny realities requires no explication for critics of the Iraq war and other recent fiascos, but the appetite for illusions remains a national as well as an organizational challenge. We entertain fantasies about our collective character: "The American people are fundamentally decent," politicians on all sides repeatedly intone—as if 300 million of us were immune to the indecencies of human nature. And we indulge in wishful thinking about our leaders. The ACLU board's deference to its executive director comports with a desire for charismatic national leadership that naturally intensifies in times of stress.

Unrealistic expectations and undue reverence for leaders plagues our personalized political life, thanks partly to the infantilizing metaphor of the nation itself as a family, headed by a parent who knows best: "The chief executive of the United States is no longer a mere constitutional officer charged with faithful execution of the laws," Gene Healy laments in his incisive critique of the cultish, imperial presidency. "He is a soul nourisher, a hope giver, a living American talisman against hurricanes, terrorism, economic downturns, and spiritual malaise. He—or she—is the one who answers the phone at 3 a.m. to keep our children safe from harm." Healy recalls a striking "vignette" from the 1992 presidential campaign: "The scene was the campaign's second televised debate, held in Richmond, Virginia; the format, a horrid Oprah-style arrangement in which a hand-picked audience of allegedly normal Americans got to lob questions at the candidates, who were perched on stools, trying to look warm and approachable. Up from the crowd popped a pony-tailed social worker named Denton Walthall, who demanded to know what George H. W. Bush, Bill Clinton, and H. Ross Perot were going to do for *us*. . . . 'I ask the three of you, how can we, as symbolically the children of the future president, expect the three of you to meet our needs, the needs in housing and in crime and you name it.'"[14]

Healy describes this episode as "little remembered," but I suspect I'm not alone in remembering it well—not just because of the unabashed childishness of Walthall's comments, but because they testified to the insidious influence of popular therapies (in 1992, the recovery movement was at its peak) and because no one reacted to Walthall's jarring vision of citizens in a democratic society as helpless children. Perhaps it was unrealistic to hope that one of the candidates would point out that he was not running for national father figure, emphasizing, however disingenuously, that he regarded voters as responsible adults. That's one lie that might actually have served a greater good.

Of course, many voters regard themselves as adults and evaluate politicians with skepticism and reason. I'm not suggesting that Dennis Walthall was speaking for all or most of us. Of course, political leaders are mocked quite mercilessly as well as revered; they're even reduced to mocking themselves on late-night TV. But the hope or hunger for the wise, benevolent leader that Healy describes is powerful; the imperial presidency was probably partly enabled by it, as he suggests. Childish voters may well be outnumbered by relatively sophisticated ones, but their influence is not necessarily neutralized.

An intense emotional longing to be led (which is not the equivalent of a desire for honorable, intelligent leadership) was evident during the 2008 primary season, especially at massive rallies for Barack Obama, who was either blessed or burdened by his image as deus ex machina. Attending an Obama rally, I was heartened by the crowd's enthusiasm for politics (as well as its expectation of defeating racism); still, the spectacle of thousands of people cheering, applauding, and apparently feeling in unison is always unnerving (even if I share their views, their fervent unanimity makes me want to change my mind). In the crush of a rope line, vying for the momentary attention or touch or even scent of a politician, people do sometimes seem a bit unhinged: "I got to smell him, and it was awesome," one Obama fan gushed to the *New York Times* during the primary campaign. "Best experience of my life," said a woman whose fingers were "pinched" by the senator.[15] Months later, Sarah Palin would evoke similar reactions from her adoring fans.

Whether or not candidates are unsettled by being objects of adoration, they exploit and encourage it by personalizing their own relationships with voters, often invoking the familial metaphor: MSNBC described Hillary Clinton at a rally in Pennsylvania, "emphasiz[ing] her role as a woman—comparing the role of a caretaker of the family to that of president of the United States. . . . 'A country is like a great big family where we have to work together,' she said, 'because we're better off if everybody's doing better.' "[16]

Personalized appeals by politicians are banal by now and, perhaps, practically mandatory, like their ubiquitous memoirs. In 2008, both Barack Obama and John McCain relied on their personal stories. Sarah Palin sought to connect with female voters who differed with her politically but liked her nonetheless, as if she were running for carpool or jogging partner instead of vice president. (Sometimes voters seem to seek imaginary friends even more than leaders.) In any case, we've surely grown accustomed to an emotive, personalized politics, which the Bush and Clinton presidencies both advanced (even as they differed greatly in tone, as well as ideology), whether the president was feeling your pain or fulfilling your desire for a beer buddy. Both asked to be liked by voters, not judged; it's fitting that both were also heartily disliked, and whether they reacted with bluster or evident self-pity, both signaled personal resentment of their critics. Extending affection to us, or a show of it, politicians implicitly solicit our affection in return. Never mind that most of us never meet them and never exist for them as individuals. ("I love you all," some pop stars assure their anonymous audiences. I doubt they expect to be taken literally, but in professing their love, they assume some responsibility for the imaginary relationships that fans, and stalkers, form with them. "You Made Me Love You," a young Judy Garland famously sings to a photo of Clark Gable in *Broadway Melody of 1938.*)

Demagogues, as well as pop stars, expertly exploit imaginary personal connections with their followers. Charismatic politicians make similar connections with voters, for better and worse, depending on their characters and resistance to abusing power. (Where the line between a charismatic and a demagogue falls is often a matter of perspective.) Franklin Roosevelt's fireside chats were exemplary, creating intimate, informal, reassuring relationships with his invisible, individual listeners: "I can hear your unspoken wonder as to where we are headed in this troubled world," he said. "He was the president, and he was talking to us, and he was going to get us out of trouble," my mother, who came of age in the Depression, recalled. In a pre-therapeutic era, Roosevelt forged his own brand of emotive, personal politics (although his chats were refreshingly free of lofty religious or spiritual appeals and replete with concrete discussions of problems and programs). But given his reliance on personality, it's not surprising that he had imperial tendencies too (which made him either a savior or aspiring dictator, depending on your politics).

Cults of personality and the irrationalism they foster naturally accompany the practice of a personalized politics and the metaphor of political and professional groups as families. Once in place, the unreasoning focus on personality is hard to reverse. It responds to a desire for leaders who don't just honor but embody collective ideals. And it's facilitated by technology. Roosevelt had radio. Today, politicians and leaders of large organizations, like the ACLU, have video. Addressing mass meetings or rallies, dwarfed by their own images projected on huge screens, even the humblest of them may feel like rock stars—celebrities who enjoy powerful emotional bonds with their families of fans. At the ACLU board, the usual familial roles were reversed: the leader—the executive director—was treated less like a father than a son, with the executive committee assuming an indulgent parental role. But the ACLU "family" still revolved around Romero's personality, which determined the dynamics of his relationship with the board and displaced concerns about his conduct. Personality eclipsed character; emotional reflexives dispatched rational analysis of facts, and like the ACLU itself, the executive director was glorified with righteous unreality.

6

Money Changes Everything

I

Some self-righteousness comes naturally to any not-for-profit group bound together by a shared vision of the public good and the group's essential role in advancing it. Board members are apt to believe that they're engaged in public service work; many derive a sense of self-importance from their organizational status, and few are easily persuaded that their presumptively altruistic group has ceased to embody its own ideals. These assumptions of virtue may partly account for a recent rise in misconduct by not-for-profit groups, noted in a 2007 report by the Ethics Resource Center. "The greatest threat to an organization is the assertion by its leaders that ethics issues 'won't happen here,'" the report observes. The ERC recommends that not-for-profit boards undergo training in ethics and oversight, stressing that "leaders must assertively communicate the importance of integrity."[1]

But it seems likely that groups convinced of their own inviolable goodness won't recognize a need for ethical training, or won't be chastened by it, until scandal makes ethical lapses undeniable. A bedrock belief in the righteousness of your group and the people who embody it isn't easily shaken or even discussed, even in a quarrelsome organization like the ACLU. While ACLU board members disagree vigorously about civil liberties issues (like First Amendment restrictions on campaign finance reform) and engage in extended debates (sometimes spending years enacting one policy), they're used to agreeing about the moral character of the ACLU and its leadership. So while the organization's policy positions remain debatable, its integrity is an article of faith.

Presuming the ACLU's integrity did indeed facilitate the sale of it. Board members who effectively precluded the possibility of core principles being compromised for money were not exactly open to considering the reality of it. Compromises were overlooked or easily rationalized, especially when they were embedded in complicated legal issues; meanwhile, the financial gains were always apparent and usually impressive. With dollar signs in your eyes it's hard to see even what's right in front of you.

As the ACLU grew rich, board members grew more reverential of riches, reversing a suspiciousness that had previously prevailed. Fifteen years ago, the national and affiliate boards debated accepting a grant from Philip Morris, out of concern for appearances and disdain for the business of selling cigarettes. We took the money in the end, but discomfort with it was not surprising. Objections to an unconditional grant from a corporation engaged in an entirely legal enterprise testified to the reflexive mistrust of money shared by many progressives, who took pride in the ability to soldier on without it.

Thirty years ago, the ACLU was impoverished. When former executive director Ira Glasser assumed office in 1978, he was confronted with a $400,000 deficit, representing over 20 percent of the ACLU's annual unrestricted income. A combination of budget cuts and a large bequest averted financial ruin, and in 1979 the ACLU hired its first development director—at a time when $500–$1,000 was considered a large gift, Glasser recalled. "Most of us . . . blanched at the prospect of asking donors for $5–10,000. . . . There was also a mistrust among some on the Board of large contributions, even from those who had been ACLU members for years. There was a feeling expressed by some that large gifts would undermine

and distort our mission."[2] The ACLU launched an endowment campaign only a decade ago, in the mid-1990s, in time
to reap the benefits of dramatically increased concentrations
of wealth and the new philanthropy it encouraged.[3]

Naturally, attitudes toward major donors changed (along
with the definition of a major gift). Wealth is easily accom-
modated, after all. I'm not lamenting the ACLU's willingness
to be enriched or the demise of disdain for money, which
enabled and expanded its work. I've never found virtue in
poverty, any more than I've found it in wealth.

But money isn't often treated as a mere, morally neutral,
commodity. Defending their wealth or compensating for the
lack of it, people tend to view money as either the root of
much evil or their reward for being good; few are likely to
believe they deserve poverty, but many consider themselves
deserving of wealth, whether they regard it as a measure of
God's grace or their own hard work and talent. Eventually,
at the ACLU, money became less a temptation than a mark of
success, and even rectitude. How could the ACLU be wrong
if it was getting rich? Wealth became symbolic of achieve-
ment and even good character—not just a subsidy for civil
liberty but a measure of the ACLU's success in protecting it.
Profit gained primacy over principle by appearing to stand
in for it.

II

Money doesn't corrupt people; people corrupt people, but
money reveals their corruptibility. The weakness for wealth
that afflicted the ACLU leadership first became apparent
in the spring of 2004, when the board inadvertently learned
that our executive director had signed a grant agreement
with the Ford Foundation including a restriction on advocacy (applied to all Ford grantees): "You agree that your organization will not promote or engage in violence, terrorism,
bigotry, or the destruction of any state."

To people dispassionate about civil liberty or unschooled

in free speech principles or First Amendment law, this language may seem harmless (and Romero staunchly defended it). But a prohibition on "promoting" violence, terrorism, bigotry, or the destruction of any state is a very broad, subjective restriction on political speech, which would be unconstitutional if applied by the government, as the ACLU would argue: enforcement of such a vague and malleable restriction on advocacy is bound to vary according to the biases of enforcers. Ford's prohibition on advocating destruction of any state (included to appease pro-Israel groups offended by the conduct of a Ford-funded Palestinian organization) could be applied to supporters of the Iraq War by progressives, who might apply the prohibition on advocating bigotry to opponents of affirmative action. Expressions of sympathy for radical antiabortion protesters or rants against U.S. policy in the Middle East might easily be prohibited as promotion of terrorism, depending on the politics of the people with prohibitory power.

That such broad, subjective restrictions on speech are inevitably imposed selectively only underscores their unfairness, unpredictability, and likely discriminatory use against political enemies. Legal prohibitions on political advocacy, similar to the Ford restrictions, were once included in criminal syndicalism statutes and used to imprison Communist Party members in the 1940s and '50s. The Supreme Court struck down these laws in 1969, holding that the most objectionable advocacy was protected speech so long as it was neither intended nor likely to incite imminent violence.[4] Ford could have met this standard by deleting its prohibition on "promoting" terrorism or violence, retaining a prohibition on "engaging" in them and deleting the references to bigotry and "destruction of any state" entirely.

The Ford restriction was an exercise in discretion; it was neither legally required nor legally impermissible. The Constitution doesn't bind a private institution, like the Ford Foundation, which enjoys its own First Amendment right to fashion its own grant agreements, and Ford may choose to restrict the constitutionally protected speech of its grantees. But that's not a choice civil libertarians would encourage or approve, and not all Ford grantees were nonchalant about the threat the new restrictions posed to controversial political advocacy.

While Romero approved the new 2004 Ford grant agreement, without informing the board, nine elite colleges and universities opposed it, citing threats to academic freedom. As a May 2004 *Wall Street Journal* article explained, university officials were concerned that "with such imprecise wording, any school-supported political or cultural activity could come under fire from one group or another. . . . Even if Ford itself doesn't want to terminate grants to a university, the new language leaves the foundation vulnerable to pressure from advocacy groups." In stark contrast, the ACLU offered a remarkably naive, ill-informed defense of the new grant restriction: "Outside the academic realm, Ford grantees said they have no problem with the new language," the *Journal* reported. "Most notably, the American Civil Liberties Union Foundation, which has four Ford grants totaling $2.3 million, said free speech isn't at risk because Ford is a private donor rather than a government agency."[5]

Reading these comments, the always alert Michael Meyers immediately jumped to the correct conclusion that Romero had signed Ford's restrictive grant agreement without informing the board. A few weeks later, at a recorded May 22, 2004, executive committee meeting, Romero acknowledged approving the Ford agreement, which he unequivocally defended. He stressed (according to the minutes) that he had "no problem signing the one grant letter and hoped to sign more" and that we should "sign this with our full conscience," noting the irrelevant fact that Ford is "entitled to decide how to spend its money." He explained that Ford had imposed its new grant restriction under pressure from Congress, perhaps not recognizing that government pressure on Ford was a reason for the ACLU to oppose the restriction on speech, not an excuse for approving it. (Speech restrictions adopted to placate government officials might be vulnerable to a constitutional challenge.) He implicitly criticized university provosts who had protested the new agreement, claiming that some of them had acted "without knowledge of their presidents." And he defended the tacit statement of support for Ford offered by an ACLU spokesperson to the *Wall Street Journal,* stating that he had purposefully avoided talking to the reporter himself, because he did not want to draw "more attention" to the new grant restriction.

Rationalizing his approval of the Ford agreement, Romero displayed, at best, insensitivity to a civil liberties issue that he may or may not have understood. But what was perhaps most striking was his desire to limit publicity or "attention" devoted to the issue—his stated concern that by talking to the reporter, he might "give much more importance" to this broad new restriction on speech affecting all of Ford's grantees than "I think it deserves."[6] Ford Foundation executives no doubt shared this concern; minimizing controversy over the new grant agreement was in Ford's interest. But—and I would have expected Romero to understand this—drawing attention to restrictions on speech is a core mission of the ACLU. I would also have expected the president and a majority of executive committee members to point this out to Romero, but when he explained his desire to squelch a free speech controversy, they listened with equanimity. With two exceptions, Michael Meyers and James Ferguson, the committee seemed untroubled that in his third year as ACLU executive director, Romero appeared to have the Ford Foundation's interests at heart.

It's only fair to add, however, that the Ford Foundation's interests in avoiding potentially embarrassing publicity coincided with the ACLU's financial interests in rationalizing approval of grant agreements restricting speech. (In the wake of 9/11, other potential ACLU funders, including the Rockefeller Foundation, incorporated speech restrictions in their grant agreements. Rockefeller would subsequently modify its restriction; Ford would not.) The ACLU had received substantial funding from Ford in the past and expected to receive more in the future. So the president and a majority of executive committee members either actively supported or declined to oppose Romero's approval of the Ford agreement. Rob Remar declared (at the May 2004 executive committee meeting) that "it was perfectly appropriate for us to sign this letter." ACLU legal director Steve Shapiro prepared a memo at the committee's request obligingly arguing that approval of the Ford agreement was consistent with ACLU policy and principles. Board president and reputed free speech advocate Nadine Strossen subsequently explained (in a June 7, 2004, conference call), "We should not see the [Ford] language as imposing restrictions. We should use the term 'conditions' instead of 'restrictions.'"[7]

With the leadership defending the agreement and advocating for approval of it (millions of dollars were at stake), a majority of board members fell in line, including those who had initially spoken out against Ford's restriction on speech.

Responding immediately to the initial *Wall Street Journal* report on the Ford agreement, one board member wrote in a May 6, 2004, e-mail that he "couldn't agree more" that "nongovernmental censorship is a significant problem," adding that the Ford agreement might reflect the foundation's concern about violating the Patriot Act. "If we could determine that this was a concern, we would have a great example of the Patriot Act's success in chilling legitimate First Amendment activities." "Never mind," he might have added two months later, when he voted with the majority to approve the agreement.

In a May 7, 2004, e-mail, another board member voiced a similar suspicion that Ford was reacting to the "thrust" of the Patriot Act, noting, "This is reminiscent of a process that became all too familiar during the McCarthy Era: repressive measures taken by the government are picked up by powerful, private institutions. The heavy-handed actions of the House Unamerican Activities Committee were copied by a number of private groups, including the Hollywood studios, who were well beyond the reach of the Constitution. . . .

Repression of free speech and academic freedom is still repression, regardless of whether it can be challenged in court." Two months later, however, the same board member belittled comparisons to McCarthyism, with no apparent recollection of having made them: "The questionable Ford grant language —and we all certainly admit it is questionable—does not by a long shot rise to the level of concern engendered by the Loyalty Oaths," he wrote to the board on July 3, 2004, adding that "any talk of returning the Ford money at this point is sheer poppycock."

Tellingly, he also suggested that those of us who disagreed and opposed approving the Ford agreement were motivated not by concerns about civil liberty but antipathy to the executive director: "The current free-for-all over the Ford Foundation grant resonates with me as perhaps part of an ongoing 'get Anthony' campaign." How can a group avoid confronting troubling, potentially costly questions about its conduct or adherence to principle? It can dismiss them as personal attacks, suppressing criticism by focusing on the presumed bad faith of critics.

Board members who voted to approve the Ford agreement, even after advocating against it, would probably point out in their defense that a few days before the July 2004 board vote, Ford president Susan Berresford sent Romero a letter generally assuring the ACLU that its civil liberty advocacy was known to Ford and would probably not violate the grant agreement: "It should not restrict the ACLU's activities as we understand them," she wrote. (Instead of amending its prohibition on political advocacy, Ford sent individual, supplemental letters like this to some concerned grantees.) But Berresford could not offer a legally binding guarantee that Ford's speech restriction would not be applied to the ACLU or other organizations that received similar supplemental letters: and having yielded to pressure from Congress (and pro-Israel lobbying groups) once, when promulgating its unnecessarily broad grant restriction, Ford might yield to similar pressure again in enforcing it.[8]

What if Berresford could have promised that the ACLU

would not be bound by the restriction on advocacy? Would her promise have justified our approval of the Ford agreement? Not if the ACLU considered itself obliged to protect the rights of other grantees, instead of simply looking after its own financial welfare. Not if the ACLU was committed to fighting what it regularly denounced as the chilling effect of the Patriot Act on political speech.

The leadership countered predictably that by enriching itself the ACLU was advancing its mission. Approving the Ford agreement would "substantially enhance the ACLU's ability to preserve civil liberty," legal director Steve Shapiro stressed in his June 4, 2004, memo. A majority of board members agreed; a significant minority dissented. The board voted to approve the agreement at its July 9, 2004, meeting by a 49 to 20 vote.

But we all voted in ignorance of a crucial fact that Romero had withheld: he had been deeply involved in formulating the grant restriction that he so ardently defended. In August 2004, a month after the board approved the agreement, Romero acknowledged to the executive committee (in response to questions I had posed months earlier) that, in his capacity as ACLU executive director, he had advised Ford to "parrot" the Patriot Act in its post 9/11 grant agreement. Having been consulted privately by Susan Berresford, he recalled, he told her to "mirror and track the language in federal law. You get outside of that and you're gonna get yourself into some difficult situations with ambiguous language that's not gonna be helpful to you. I would just parrot back language in existing federal law. If you're worried about protecting any accusations that you're funding terrorism, which is one of their concerns, I said re-parrot what is required under the Patriot Act."[9] Acknowledging his role in covertly advancing the influence of the Patriot Act while the ACLU was raising millions of dollars opposing it, Romero sounded proud that Ford's president had turned to him (and a few other important people) for advice. He sounded defiant in admitting that he told her to mirror the Patriot Act, as if he were flaunting his prerogative to act in contempt of the ACLU's mission, without ever being held to account.

He did seem to enjoy immunity: neither the executive committee nor the full board expressed surprise or disapproval, much less consternation, on learning of Romero's advice to Berresford and what can only have been his intentional concealment of it prior to the board vote, when he was explicitly asked about his role in crafting Ford's new agreement. Some members had the questionable excuse of ignorance, even after the executive director's advice to Ford was exposed in the *New York Times*.[10] Several people privately reported being assured by members of the executive committee that Romero had not, in fact, said what the *Times* reported he had said, and what the tape and executive committee minutes recorded. The ACLU press office spun the *Times* report in its January 21, 2005, talking points, distributed throughout the organization: "What Anthony told the Ford Foundation is nothing but the truth: that whether we like it or not, the Patriot Act is law. Despite our strong beliefs that aspects of the law are wrong, foundations often summarize relevant legal obligations for grantees in their grant letters." The first claim was inaccurate (if Romero's description of his advice were true); the second was misleading, since the Ford restriction on advocacy was not a summary of the "relevant legal obligations for grantees." It was an extralegal obligation, imposed at Ford's discretion.

Romero's advice to Ford was quite difficult to excuse openly; so it was covered up or simply ignored. Even the two unwittingly prescient board members who had warned that the Ford restrictions reflected the influence of the Patriot Act appeared untroubled by Romero's complicity in spreading it or by the threats to free speech that they had stressed in their initial e-mails to the board. Both voted with the leadership to authorize approval of the Ford agreement twice—once before and once after they learned about Romero's role in crafting it. Both were subsequently elected to the ACLU's executive committee.

———

In the end, despite all these machinations, the leadership lost the battle to accept Ford funding, by the narrowest of margins: an October 17, 2004 vote to withdraw approval of the Ford agreement ended in a tie, which for procedural reasons decided the issue in favor of withdrawal. (Strossen, Susan Herman, and a majority of executive members voted to approve the Ford restriction.) But the board's reversal did not reflect concern about Romero's advice to Ford, which was generally ignored. It was a reaction to an embarrassing, front-page *New York Times* story by Adam Liptak, exposing Romero's complicity with what the ACLU officially regarded as government blacklisting: "The American Civil Liberties Union is in turmoil over a promise it made to the government that it would not knowingly hire people whose names appear on watch lists of suspected supporters of terrorism," the *Times* reported on July 31, 2004. "Those lists are the very type it has strongly opposed in other contexts."[11]

Why would Romero voluntarily promise to boycott people named on the watch lists? He did it for money, in order to participate in the Combined Federal Campaign (CFC), a charitable-giving program for federal employees from which the ACLU usually reaped about $500,000 a year. After 9/11, to qualify as a CFC-approved charity, organizations were required to sign a contract promising not to employ anyone named on the post-9/11 watch lists. A majority of Americans might applaud the Bush administration for demanding this promise and charitable organizations for offering it. But it was an obvious exercise in hypocrisy for the ACLU, analogous to the now infamous loyalty oath the organization adopted in 1940. The ACLU vehemently opposed use of the lists (and was publicizing its opposition to screening airline passengers against watch lists at the same time that Romero was quietly agreeing to screen ACLU employees). From a civil libertarian perspective, and according to the rhetoric, if not the actions of the ACLU, "watch list" was a euphemism for "blacklist."

Romero signed the CFC agreement in relative secret and concealed it from the board for some six months, during discussions of post-9/11 funding restrictions. He may not have sympathized with the ACLU's official dismay at the watch lists, but he was obviously sufficiently aware of it to fear exposure. (The ACLU's public opposition to the lists, like its private promise to comply with them, was one of his fundraising tools.) The board didn't learn about Romero's promise to consult the watch lists until after its approval of the Ford grant restrictions at the July 2004 meeting, when bits of information about the CFC watch-list agreement that Romero had buried in a lengthy memo were finally uncovered. Romero defended his approval of the CFC agreement (after acknowledging it in response to direct questions), stating that he had not checked any lists, had no intention of checking any lists, and did not believe that he was required to check any lists by his promise not to hire people named on them. Nadine Strossen seemed neither surprised nor concerned by Romero's approval and concealment of the CFC agreement, and the board reacted to it placidly: Michael Meyers made a motion to withdraw from the CFC; Strossen, presiding over the meeting, made a ruling cutting off debate on his motion, and it was voted down resoundingly.

Imagine the pope endorsing abortion rights. Imagine the head of the NRA secretly supporting a prohibition on handguns or the head of a gay-rights group quietly opposing gay marriage. Romero's covert approval of the watch lists was a similar betrayal—which the board declined to condemn or, when given the chance, immediately correct.

III

The CFC debacle (which had only begun) was a watershed in the ACLU's decline. It required the board to rationalize or ignore the intentional violation of a core civil liberties principle, not just a few "fibs" about internal governance. It showed how group solidarity and suppression of dissent can

undermine group ethics and loyalty to core ideals. It dramatized the relationship between integrity in governance and
effectiveness in carrying out a mission—in this case the preservation of civil liberties and opposition to post-9/11 excesses,
like the use of notoriously inaccurate, ineffective watch lists
and the onerous, arbitrary regulation of not-for-profit organizations. The post-9/11 legal regime, reflected in CFC certification requirements and the Ford grant restrictions on
speech and association, poses gratuitous harm to "charitable
organizations and the people they serve," as OMB Watch
and Grantmakers without Borders documented in an extensive 2008 report. (In an apparent excess of team spirit, however, the report whitewashed the ACLU's complicity with the
post-9/11 restrictions it so persuasively critiqued.)[12]

The ACLU could have challenged the legality of watch-
list laws cited by the CFC; instead it chose to pledge compliance with them, quietly. In fact, at an August 2004 executive
committee meeting, held shortly after exposure of the watch-
list agreement, legal director Steve Shapiro cautioned against
challenging the government's power to maintain the lists,
while Romero stated (according to the minutes), "We don't
want our enemies to think that we oppose any attempts to
participate in anti-terrorism." (A legal case against the watch-
list laws would be initiated by the Center for Constitutional
Rights,[13] which also began organizing the defense of Guantánamo detainees early in 2002, while the ACLU dithered.)

But by July 2004, when Romero confessed that he had
signed the CFC agreement back in January, the ACLU board
was already committed to the path it had chosen a year earlier
when first confronted with evidence of the executive director's misconduct. The executive committee and a majority of
the board reacted reflexively, ignoring his failure to disclose
the agreement and treating his approval of it like another
administrative faux pas or proverbial "teachable moment"; a
few people, including the board president, defended it.

"I think it is quite clear to old civil liberties hands that
we should not have done this—we need to understand that

it wasn't so obvious to a newbie," a long-serving board member asserted in a July 11, 2004, e-mail, acknowledging that Romero's approval of the CFC agreement was not "acceptable," while dismissing it as another "error" and ignoring its concealment. The speciousness of this popular argument confirmed the decreasing relevance of facts: the "newbie" had been the ACLU's executive director for about three years; he was trained as a lawyer; he was hired because of his alleged familiarity with civil liberties and had been raising money based on his stated opposition to the 9/11 watch lists and other controversial antiterror laws; opposition to the watch lists was hardly an obscure, technical matter that only "old civil liberties hands" would appreciate.

In fact, while Romero was being defended as a new guy with a learning curve, he was also being praised for his strategic acumen in signing a blacklist agreement and then claiming that it did not oblige him to engage in blacklisting. "Anthony's actions strike me as a very sophisticated form of 'civil disobedience,'" another lawyer on the board wrote. "He gets the money to help the ACLU continue fighting Ashcroft, the Patriot Act, and the rest of the true enemies of civil liberties, while neutralizing the attempt to increase the use of the lists."

Civil disobedience? Not quite. Civil disobedience is an intentionally public protest, an intentionally public submission to prosecution for an intentionally public violation of arguably unjust laws, not a strategy for secretly subverting them. Romero's sneakiness did not remotely resemble civil disobedience. He didn't chop down a cherry tree in daylight and readily confess his offense. He chopped it down at night, and then, with no apparent intention of confessing in the morning, ran into the kitchen to make a cherry pie.

If Romero's approval of the CFC agreement wasn't civil disobedience, did it still reflect a "sophisticated" interpretation of the requirement that the ACLU "does not knowingly employ individuals or contribute funds to organizations" named on specified watch lists? Romero explained that he had interpreted the phrase "knowingly employ" to mean that he was only required to screen employees against the lists if he took the trouble to read them.

This is not a sophisticated interpretation; it's a desperate one. (My colleague Harvey Silverglate, a criminal defense attorney for forty years, remarked to me that any lawyer who advised his client to rely on Romero's interpretation of the CFC agreement could be guilty of malpractice.) As several attorneys on the ACLU board pointed out (often in private), when Romero confessed, on tape, that he had promised not to employ anyone named on specified lists with no intention of ever actually screening employees against the lists, he exposed himself to prosecution under a federal frauds statute. "Purposefully failing to read the blacklist and then certifying that we have not knowingly employed someone on the list could lead to criminal or civil liability on behalf of the organization," one board member cautioned in a July 30, 2004, e-mail to the full board. "The courts have long recognized the willful blindness doctrine. It allows a 'jury to impute the element of knowledge to [a] defendant if the evidence indicates that he purposely closed his eyes to avoid knowing what was taking place around him.'"

The chances that Romero or the ACLU would be prosecuted for his little ploy seemed remote, but, this board member added, "The question should not be is it possible to interpret the language in a way that allows us to get the money but not commit perjury." What troubled her was Romero's implicit "message" of approval for the watch lists. "I find it highly unlikely that the federal employees, other charities which participate in the campaign, and other folks are assuming that we're playing games with words so we can have our cake and eat it too."

ACLU president Nadine Strossen was apparently unconcerned about the "message" sent by Romero and unpersuaded that he had erred in approving the CFC watch-list agreement (much less engaged in misconduct by concealing it). Instead, she found his actions praiseworthy, as the *New York Times* reported: Strossen "said Mr. Romero's decision to sign the certification was based on a 'very reasonable, certainly clever interpretation. Do we do more harm than good by spurning money by certifying something that is plausible but not the only plausible interpretation?' she asked. 'It's completely a debate about strategy, not principle. I think Anthony handled it completely appropriately.' "[14]

But Strossen was alone in defending Romero's action to the *Times*; other executive committee members conceded that Romero had erred and the *Times* story reportedly generated immediate protests from donors and members. So on the day the story appeared, July 31, the ACLU withdrew from the CFC, rescinding the agreement that the board had declined to rescind three weeks earlier, with Strossen's implicit support.

Public exposure of the ACLU's agreement with the CFC generated much more angst and action than Romero's acknowledgment of the agreement to the ACLU board on July 9, 2004. People who quickly dismissed Romero's actions as understandable mistakes, or lauded them as clever strategies, quickly condemned those of us suspected of "leaking" the CFC story to the *Times* (mainly me and Michael Meyers). It's no secret that we talked to *Times* reporter Adam Liptak (along with other critics), but we did not "leak" the CFC story: it was public information, and not just because it involved the ACLU's participation in a government program for federal employees. The July 2004 meeting at which Romero admitted approving the CFC agreement, which the board then declined to rescind, was open to the public and press (like most ACLU board meetings; only executive sessions are closed); it coincided with a general membership meeting and was attended by people who were not members of the board. Still, exposure of the CFC agreement was treated like the leak of a state secret; the leakers were derided on the board Listserv as "whistlepunks," attacked for their "petulence [*sic*], a lack of collegiality, and a disregard for democratic processes," and exhorted to resign from the board; I was compared to a "pregnant sow" harboring a "squealing unborn piglet."

Meanwhile, board members praised Romero for deftly

handling the bad publicity generated by the "leak": "I do want to congratulate Anthony and [his communications director] on the rapid response to the crisis created by the NY Times article. It was truly a spectacular mobilization of forces," one board member wrote on August 1, 2004, the day after the *Times* story appeared. Another joined her "in congratulating Anthony, Emily, and other staff for what they were able to do with this media fiasco. They turned something negative into something positive and focused on the real problem!" The applause was a response to an August 1, 2004, "status report" from Romero trumpeting his success in spinning the story: "Well, what a difference a day makes! Below you will find several articles that describe the actions we took yesterday and a marked shift in media coverage. . . . I have also contacted most of our largest contributors. For example, in my breakfast with Peter Lewis this morning, he complimented our handling of the situation—though he was troubled about how the situation arose."

Not everyone joined in the chorus of attacks on me and Meyers, or in the plaudits for Romero; a few people gently dissented in public and others less gently in private. But the prevailing view, reflected in numerous e-mails and conversations, was that Romero had made another innocent mistake, which his critics were guilty of exploiting in order to embarrass him and the organization, out of vindictiveness, egoism, or some other pathology.

This was the story line adopted by the executive committee when it met on August 7, 2004, a week after the *Times* article about the watch-list agreement appeared. The meeting was marked by anger at the suspected whistlepunks and sympathy for Romero, who condemned the "small group" of people who "were more interested in advancing their own personal agenda than in advancing the interest of the ACLU," even as he apologized for his "mistake." He was immediately and effusively forgiven. Committee members applauded when Roz Litman declared, "The public relations disaster that could have been was only averted because of

the incredibly devoted and wonderful work of the staff." Rob
Remar praised Romero "for his forthrightness in apologizing and acknowledging the error in judgment," and stressed
that "everyone I've talked to thinks that Anthony and the
staff have done an incredible job and are exasperated over
the constant attacks." Contacting the *Times* was "reprehen-
sible," Remar added, but he smartly advised taking no overt,
official action against the suspect board members.[15] Remar,
among other executive committee members, also claimed
at this August meeting that Romero had sent the CFC certification language including the watch-list requirement to
the executive committee two months earlier, in June 2004,
implying that he had not withheld information about it (although he had signed the agreement in January). But even
this claim would soon be qualified, since it raised questions
about the executive committee's complicity in concealing the
agreement from the board. Remar subsequently insisted in
an e-mail that he had not known that Romero had approved
the CFC language until he acknowledged doing so at the
July 2004 board meeting.

Covering for Romero's secretiveness and trivializing his
"error" in signing the CFC agreement—"He's making one
mistake a year, which is not a bad batting average," Susan
Herman observed—the executive committee also minimized
the harm of post-9/11 watch lists to individuals and organizations (which other advocacy groups would eventually document).[16] Milton Estes complained that Romero's apology for
approving the CFC agreement was excessive: "It wasn't a co-
lossal blunder," Estes declared. "Nothing terrible happened
[because of it] except by dint of someone going to the *New
York Times*. . . . That's the bad thing that happened."[17]

Given this analysis of the "crisis" facing the ACLU, it's
not surprising that the solution proposed by Romero and the
executive committee was a purge of Meyers and me. Turning
off the tape recorder, the committee went into a closed session ostensibly to discuss "personnel matters," but according
to Meyers, who was present, the session focused on strategies

for expelling us or defeating us electorally, asserting that we had "hijacked" the organization. ("They talked about me as if I weren't there," Meyers told me.) Among friends, Romero declared that his critics could "kiss my Hispanic ass," according to Meyers. Romero later corrected this account, reporting he had said we could "kiss his Puerto Rican ass."

I don't mean to suggest that anger over the *New York Times* story was merely a cynical distraction from the conduct that provoked it. The anger was genuine, and it was shared by some people who were disturbed by Romero's handling of the CFC agreement and did not regard it as an entirely innocent mistake (although they seemed resigned to what they privately acknowledged was a pattern of misconduct, as if they lacked the power to address it). The belief that a board of directors is obliged to prevent, not facilitate, exposure of embarrassing or even unethical missteps is imprinted on most board members; as a general rule, it's appropriate. Are there exceptions? Many board members acknowledge, in theory, that exposure may be justified in some circumstances—when the missteps are sufficiently serious or illegal and the organization seems intent on not correcting them. But in practice, few will recognize that such circumstances exist. In theory, the ACLU values whistle-blowing, and in practice the ACLU defends whistle-blowing, when directed against the government or presumptively corrupt private institutions. But it's difficult, or virtually impossible, for many ACLU loyalists to imagine that whistle-blowing might ever be necessary or justified at the ACLU, which is presumed to embody the virtues that it's devoted to instilling in government—the fair, open, and honest use of power that respects individual freedom, particularly freedom of speech. By challenging the ACLU's claim to these virtues, whistle-blowing denies the ACLU its raison d'être.

So I don't minimize the threat posed by our criticisms or deride the fear and anger generated by publicizing the ACLU's apparent hypocrisies. That Romero's acknowledg-

ment of the CFC agreement and the board's refusal to rescind it occurred at a public meeting eased the decision to
speak publicly; neither I nor other critics who talked to a *New
York Times* reporter had to confront the ethical dilemmas of
whistle-blowers who divulge confidential information. But
the nonconfidential nature of the CFC story was, in effect,
permission to discuss it with the press, not a reason to do so.
Why air it publicly? Romero's approval and concealment of
what civil libertarians considered a government blacklisting
agreement was no minor misstep. The board had rejected an
opportunity to remedy it and generally seemed anxious to
add the CFC matter to the list of minor "errors" that it had
previously declined to remedy or even recognize. Internal
governance debates and internal oversight had been deeply,
perhaps irrevocably, compromised, and the ACLU's post-9/11
work—the excuse for ignoring Romero's "mistakes"—was being compromised in turn. ACLU members were being misled. Even if the CFC agreement were eventually rescinded
(an uncertain prospect), it seemed likely to be rescinded as
quietly as it had been approved; members and donors who
supported the ACLU in the belief that it vehemently opposed post-9/11 watch lists would probably never have been
told that it had volunteered to abide by them.

The ACLU leadership had developed the habit of discrediting and discouraging dissent partly by countering it
with misinformation, which was disseminated vigorously to
donors, ACLU national and affiliate boards, and the media
in reaction to the *Times* CFC story. (The ACLU immediately
hired former Carter administration press secretary Jody
Powell to help manage the PR "crisis" the story created.)
"Fibs" abounded, notably Romero's frequently repeated reference to his lawyer's alleged advice that a promise not to
hire anyone named on the watch lists imposed no obligation
to check the lists. In fact, Romero did not obtain counsel's
advice until some six months after he signed the CFC agreement, at about the time he heard from Adam Liptak of the
Times. In fact, as the attorney I consulted observed, he mis-

characterized or misunderstood the advice from counsel that he belatedly solicited. The opinion letter from outside counsel made clear that Romero had assumed a legal obligation to screen employees against the watch lists and that his announced intention not to do so potentially exposed him and the organization to federal criminal prosecution. Strossen and Romero tried unsuccessfully to conceal counsel's letter from the board, but their efforts proved unnecessary: when the letter was eventually released to the board (after a brief fracas), Romero's mischaracterization of it, which entailed a mischaracterization of the ACLU's potential criminal and civil liability, was studiously ignored.[18]

Fostering the misapprehension that he had relied on counsel's advice in approving the CFC agreement, Romero continued professing surprise that he was required to check the watch lists merely because he had promised not to hire anyone named on them (as if his offense lay merely in promising to read the watch lists, not in promising to boycott people they targeted, however mistakenly). In a report to the board on August 1, 2004, he claimed, falsely, implausibly, and indignantly that he was unaware the government "expected us to actually check our employees against the terrorism lists" until he read the government's interpretation of the CFC agreement in the *New York Times* (although the *Times* quoted Romero disputing that interpretation). "Legal advice provided to the ACLU indicates that it is reasonable in our interpretation that we were not required to check those lists," Romero stated in an August 1, 2004, interview on National Public Radio's *Morning Edition*. "[And] now today, we wake up this morning and we open the newspapers and we read from the head of the Combined Federal Campaign that they want us to check those lists."

A few days later, however, on August 7, Romero told a different story to the ACLU executive committee; off the air and out of public view as well as the earshot of donors, he ceased professing surprise at the CFC watch-list requirement cited in the *Times* and reported discussing that requirement with CFC officials before the *Times* story appeared. He casually explained that he had submitted his initial CFC application months earlier without checking off the provision requiring compliance with watch lists, which a staffer had flagged for him. When his application was rejected as incomplete, and with about $500,000 a year at stake, he reconsidered: without benefit of counsel's advice, he decided that he could not be charged with "knowingly" hiring people named on the watch lists if he never read them; most tellingly, he reviewed the list of other organizations participating in the CFC and decided that they would provide the ACLU with "cover."

The great majority of executive committee members, including the president, didn't seem to mind that instead of doing the right thing (from a civil liberties perspective), the executive director was intent on seeking cover for what was obviously wrong. As Romero gradually reshaped the organization in his image, with the support of lay leaders, purging the board and staff (making clear the costs of dissenting, or being suspected of sympathizing with dissenters), the ACLU focused increasingly on maintaining its "cover," or the appearance of loyalty to civil liberties principles it was actively betraying.

Cover stories were quickly concocted in the wake of the CFC exposé. Convincing board members, donors, and supporters, as well as the ACLU board (which was passive but not yet comatose), that Romero's approval of the CFC agreement was an understandable mistake and "nothing terrible happened except that someone went to the *Times*," required considerable fictionalizing. In establishing his innocent-mistake defense, Romero repeatedly peddled the false claim that he had relied on counsel's advice in signing the CFC agreement (two years later, even he was no longer making that claim with a straight face, instead admitting, with a "sheepish grin," that he had acted as his own counsel).[19] But having voted down a motion to rescind the CFC agreement when it was exposed, at the July 9 meeting, the board needed cover as well, and Strossen supplied it.

In an August 7, 2004, e-mail to the board, Strossen blithely rewrote very recent history: recalling the July 9 board meeting, she described what never actually occurred: "At our July Board meeting, you passed motions that directed Anthony to review our options with the CFC," Strossen wrongly reminded us. (The tape and minutes of the meeting confirm that the board passed no such motions.)[20] A few days later, on August 12, Strossen sent a letter to ACLU state affiliate presidents offering additional fictions about the July 2004 national board meeting (fictions that were probably circulated to donors): she claimed that the board had "delegated responsibility to its Executive Committee . . . to consider [the CFC requirements] and to propose further steps during its next meeting, on August 7th." (Again, the record confirms that the board did no such thing.) Strossen falsely denied that the board had rejected a motion to withdraw from the CFC, stating that "the Board did not take any final action either approving or disapproving the staff's interpretation of the CFC certification requirements" and that the *Times* had "mischaracterized a discussion of the [CFC] issue," although, once again, to my knowledge, no request for a correction was ever made—perhaps because the *Times* report was accurate and confirmed by the tape and minutes of the meeting.

What is perhaps most striking about these little cover stories, apart from their boldness, are their obvious inconsistencies. It's likely that most people were not paying attention to the details (much less checking Strossen's claims against the record), but many also seemed content if not eager to be misled. When details and proofs of official falsehoods were outlined for the board, they were generally ignored, if not met with resentment and ire. Serving happily on the ACLU board began to require stubborn ignorance, or the willing suspension of disbelief.

Take the foolish, easily falsifiable claim (repeated by Strossen) that the ACLU "learned for the first time, in a July 31 *New York Times* article" about the government's expectation that a promise not to hire people named on the watch lists entailed a promise to check the lists. Anyone who read the article with any care would know that this claim was false, since it included Romero's objection to that precise expectation. But even more disconcerting is the confidence or obliviousness with which Strossen contradicts this claim as soon as she makes it: her August 12, 2004, letter stating that the ACLU first learned about the CFC's interpretation of its requirements from the *New York Times* article also complains that the article "short-circuited" the ACLU's efforts to challenge those requirements. In other words, according to Strossen, prior to July 31, 2004, the ACLU was formulating a challenge to screening requirements of which it was ignorant until July 31, 2004. Go figure, you might say on reading this, but no one did.

Am I "nitpicking," as apologists for the ACLU leadership used to claim? Strossen's misstatements about the board's responses to the CFC watch-list agreement may appear trivial, even unintended. Viewed in isolation, small, narrative discrepancies often seem and often are innocent and unimportant. But sometimes small discrepancies accumulate, forming patterns that reveal their deceptive power and purpose. Collectively, Strossen's misstatements (and those of other staff and lay leaders) were essential face-saving, fundraising fictions that reassured donors and allowed board members to avoid acknowledging that they were tolerating obvious misconduct and violations of fundamental civil liberties principles—including, not so incidentally, the honesty, transparency, and tolerance for dissent that were supposed to govern the ACLU internally.

"Fibbing" got Romero into trouble initially, but fibbing would also get him out of it, along with Strossen and other lay leaders. What sustained the ACLU leadership in the midst of scandal—news about the CFC agreement as well as Romero's long-concealed advice to Ford to "parrot" the Patriot Act—was the alternate reality that a series of small misstatements successfully constructed.

7

Potemkin Villages

I

Tolerating a series of cover stories, or lies, that helped enrich the ACLU and protect it from embarrassing, potentially costly publicity, the board oversaw the establishment of a public relations campaign that gradually began to replace some of the important post-9/11 work it was supposed to enable. Appearances began to matter most, especially to the self-aggrandizing leaders, mainly Romero and Strossen. There are multiple ironies in the ACLU story, not the least of which is that by obeying its herd instinct in shunning internal critics, the ACLU board protected the reputations and advanced the individual agendas of its leaders, not the collective mission of the organization.

By the fall of 2004, the furor over Romero's approval of the Combined Federal Campaign agreement had dissipated. Romero even managed to turn the CFC controversy to his advantage: a few months after withdrawing from the CFC in reaction to embarrassing publicity, the ACLU filed a lawsuit purportedly challenging the requirement that organizations participating in the CFC refrain from hiring people named on the post-9/11 watch lists. Announcing the litigation administered a small dose of favorable publicity and later provided an excuse for the ACLU to renew its CFC participation, but the lawsuit did not, in fact, challenge the watch-list requirement and would become the subject of yet another dispute in the fall of 2005.

The misrepresentation of our lawsuit against the CFC was perhaps the most troubling of all the known offenses by the ACLU leadership that occurred during my tenure on the board: in addition to signaling the primacy of public relations even over litigation, it facilitated the ACLU's complicity with post-9/11 watch-list laws it pretended to oppose, while smaller, poorer civil liberties groups actually exposed and opposed them. But this most troubling of offenses was also most obscure; understanding it required understanding a web of federal laws that was invisible to most of us.

Most Americans are probably unaware that, after 9/11, every time they bought a bagel or a pair of shoes, tipped a waiter, or hired anyone to perform any personal or professional service, they risked violating federal antiterror laws. Shortly after 9/11, all U.S. persons (including all charities, businesses, and individuals) were prohibited from engaging in any economic transactions with anyone named on extensive and notoriously inaccurate federal watch lists. If you violated the watch-list laws unintentionally, you could incur a substantial civil penalty; in addition, your name could be added to the lists, meaning that no one would be permitted to engage in any transactions with you. Once named, you'd officially become an economic nonperson: your assets could be frozen and you could be denied any right to support yourself or receive charity. The government assumed the authority to investigate and include you on the list without providing notice and an opportunity to challenge your designation as a terrorist.

Of course, these laws were not applied to all innocent, incidental transactions. How could they have been? But they were applied arbitrarily. How could they not have been? A 2007 report by the Lawyer's Committee for Civil Rights chronicled the harm posed by the watch lists to ordinary, unsuspecting Americans who were denied credit, jobs, and housing (as well as the right to fly) because they were wrongly included on the lists or because their names were similar to those of others on the lists.[1] The Center for Constitutional

Rights directly challenged the legality of the post-9/11 watch lists.[2] This was essentially the challenge that the ACLU had expressly declined to bring, when (in 2004) Romero and ACLU legal director Steve Shapiro cautioned the executive committee against suing the government for maintaining the watch lists. It was essentially the challenge that the ACLU pretended to mount in its case against the CFC.

What did the ACLU case against the CFC actually entail? The ACLU sued the CFC because its agreement with charities recited federal legal prohibitions on hiring or supporting people named on government watch lists.[3] The case was settled when the CFC agreed to substitute a shorthand reference to these prohibitions for an explicit recital of them: in other words, instead of requiring charities to certify that that they did not "knowingly employ individuals or contribute funds to organizations" named in specified lists, the CFC agreement would simply require charities to certify that they were "in compliance" with specified federal laws, without explicitly stating that these laws prohibited hiring or contributing funds to anyone named in specified lists. This settlement did not exempt charities from watch-list requirements that the ACLU led people to believe it had successfully challenged. The CFC simply incorporated by reference a requirement that it had previously spelled out.

The ACLU lawsuit was cosmetic: it succeeded in making implicit a watch-list requirement that had previously been explicit. But it was marketed as a victory against blacklisting. A November 9, 2005, press release declared that as a result of the ACLU lawsuit, the CFC would no longer require "that all participating charities check their employees and expenditures against several government watch lists for 'terrorist activities' and that organizations certify that they do not contribute funds to organizations on those lists." This was, at best, a Clintonian statement—technically true, in part, but entirely misleading. It was true that the CFC would no longer explicitly require charities to check the watch lists (federal law did not include an explicit list-checking requirement), but it was also true that charities would still be prohibited from hiring or otherwise supporting anyone named on the lists. In other words, organizations that managed to deduce or intuit the content of the watch lists without reading them and then boycotted anyone named in them could still be in compliance with the law.

In the new ACLU, this qualified as triumph for civil liberties: in the November 9, 2005, press release, Romero hailed it as "a major victory for non-profit organizations that refused to be subjected to vague government requirements forcing us to become law enforcement officers for the federal government." Anyone reading this who assumed the truthfulness of ACLU press releases (as ACLU members were likely to do) would wrongly believe that charities participating in the CFC were no longer required to comply with watch-list laws. I believed as much until I read the legal papers in our lawsuit and the new CFC regulations; then even I was surprised, having assumed that litigation was still sacred and accounts of the nature and effect of our lawsuits were true.

So I distributed the new CFC rules in an e-mail to the national board, questioning the extent of our "major victory." The response was predictable. One board member chastised me for conveying my "opinions" in e-mails that were "not official methods for communicating about ACLU governing matters," and engaging in "unending and unjustified personal attacks on Anthony. . . . Wendy does a good job of continuing to drag a few board members into 'discussions' by mixing potentially 'valid' comments and thoughts with her unending unjustified accusations." One executive committee member e-mailed the usual plea: "CAN'T WE JUST PLEASE MOVE ON???"

And move on we did, without first confronting the deceptiveness of our lawsuit and claims of success. The board accepted Romero's characterization of the CFC "victory," even after learning what it comprised. (A memo from staff subsequently confirmed my analysis.) In January 2006, by a substantial majority, the board authorized Romero to approve the new, essentially unimproved CFC agreement, understanding that it was authorizing him to pledge our compliance with federal watch-list laws, but reasoning that we were bound by the laws whether or not we signed the CFC agreement. That's true, but we were not bound to signal our approval of laws that we condemned by volunteering to comply with them, for money. And by volunteering our compliance, we were risking additional liability for noncompliance, if we were found to have intentionally misled the government when we promised to obey the law. As Martha Stewart might attest, it's a crime to lie to federal officials. Romero assured the board, and reportedly informed the government, that he would not check the watch lists, leaving unanswered questions about how he intended to keep his promise to boycott anyone named on them and continue to qualify for CFC funds.

This debacle, like the fracas over the Ford grant agreement, left little question that fundraising was driving policy, practice, and rationalizations for unprincipled conduct at the ACLU. One veteran board member repeatedly argued that the ACLU had an obligation to approve the CFC agreement, and other funding restrictions offensive to civil libertarians, in order to frustrate a conspiracy to "de-fund the left." In other words, hypocrisy was not simply a tolerable vice but a virtue: the ACLU was obliged to violate the principles for which it stood in order to protect them. And having betrayed civil liberties only to preserve them, it could also denounce the abusive practices with which it had quietly complied. "Terrorist Watch List Hits One Million Names," the ACLU protested in a July 14, 2008, press release, criticizing the lack of due process afforded people named on the lists and announcing "the creation of an online form where victims of the watch lists can tell us their stories" (which would presumably not include complaints that the ACLU had profited from its voluntary pledge of allegiance to the watch-list laws). Whether or not this public education campaign would help check watch-list abuses, it would surely help cover for the ACLU's complicity with them. The legal story of the ACLU's entanglement with the watch lists was complicated, but the appearance of its consistent opposition to them was clear.

The ACLU became increasingly theatrical, as the leadership produced little civil liberties plays to obscure its abandonment of big civil liberties issues, including, most notably, the detentions at Guantánamo Bay. One of the most glaring acts of omission during the post-9/11 era, either unacknowledged or unnoticed by the board, was the ACLU's failure to help provide representation for detainees when the Bush administration consigned them to the Guantánamo detention center in early 2002. The small, financially insecure Center for Constitutional Rights (CCR) took the lead in fighting for the rights of detainees, when chances of prevailing legally or in the arena of public relations seemed slim. The ACLU had joined CCR in suing the government for summarily detaining twelve hundred immigrants in the United States immediately after 9/11, but CCR was left fighting for the rights of Guantánamo detainees alone. A 2006 profile of CCR president Michael Ratner reported: "When Ratner filed habeas petitions on behalf of three Guantánamo detainees in the spring of 2002, his work got lonely. 'We found three or four death penalty lawyers willing to help us, and that was it,' Ratner says. 'Human rights groups wouldn't touch it.'"[4]

As Guantánamo became a cause célèbre for civil libertarians, the ACLU sent "observers" there; it railed against deprivations of due process and filed Freedom of Information Act requests regarding the treatment of U.S. prisoners; it invoked Guantánamo in fundraising campaigns and eventually sought detainees to defend. But, a staff member reported to me, "by the time we got around to it, all the high-profile cases were gone."

Then several years later, in 2008, the administration announced its intention to try seven "high value" detainees on capital charges. High value implied high profile; so in April

2008, over six years after the establishment of the Guantánamo prison camps, the ACLU announced the assemblage
of a "dream team" of attorneys to intervene in high-value
cases.[5] Romero partnered with the National Association of
Criminal Defense Lawyers (NACDL) to organize the dream
team, explaining to the ACLU executive committee that the
NACDL could accept grants from the Ford Foundation that
the board had barred the ACLU from accepting (and that
he had arranged a meeting between NACDL and Ford).
The ACLU heralded the assemblage of its dream team in a
lengthy self-congratulatory statement that lingered long on
its homepage and became the centerpiece of a multimillion-
dollar fundraising campaign. The initiative was called the
John Adams Project.

Why John Adams? The Guantánamo initiative was announced shortly after the airing of a heavily promoted,
seven-part HBO series on Adams that burnished his reputation and established his brand. Adams may seem like an odd
mascot for the ACLU, given his support for the notorious
Alien and Sedition Acts, pursuant to which he imprisoned
his critics, but early in his career, he had represented British soldiers charged with killing colonials during a riot in
Boston in 1770. So, associating itself with Adams, the ACLU
declared, "We simply cannot stand by and allow the Bush
Administration's military commissions to make a mockery
of our Constitution and our values. . . . We believe that we
must step into the fray . . . like John Adams who defended
the British soldiers." The analogy was misleading: unlike
Adams, the ACLU wasn't actually defending any detainees
when it announced this initiative and sought millions of dollars to support it. Romero did try hard to enlist clients: in
early June 2008, two months after announcing the John Adams Project, when the government commenced proceedings
against "high value" detainees, Romero reportedly traveled
to Guantánamo in an unsuccessful effort to persuade Khalid
Shaikh Mohammed and codefendants to accept representation by ACLU-affiliated attorneys. Undeterred by their refus-

als, the ACLU continued boasting of its alleged intervention in the military commissions trials, as if it were boldly going where no organization had gone before.

If only this initiative had been presented forthrightly as a more modest effort to assist military attorneys assigned to represent alleged terrorists in capital cases, with an acknowledgment that other organizations and attorneys had spent years fighting for the due process rights of detainees. I don't doubt the passion or sincerity of the capital-defense attorneys involved in the John Adams Project, and I assume that their assistance was welcomed by military attorneys (and may eventually be welcomed by some detainees).[6] If only their initial status as advisers had been clearly conveyed to ACLU supporters and the press. While the ACLU carefully included in its PR materials the technical truth that it was organizing lawyers to assist in representing detainees, the distinction between advising their assigned attorneys and actually representing detainees was buried by rhetoric about the ACLU's courage in challenging the military commissions. Not surprisingly, the fact that the John Adams Project lacked clients was effectively ignored even by savvy reporters. "The ACLU is spearheading a high-profile effort to defend . . . alleged 9/11 conspirators," the *Wall Street Journal* reported on April 4, 2008.[7] The headline for the *Journal* article was a little more subdued, declaring, "ACLU to Back-Up Defense of 9/11 Detainees." So, in a subsequent fundraising appeal, the ACLU distributed what purported to be an accurate copy of the article, with a more aggrandizing headline: "ACLU Leads Defense Effort for Alleged 9/11 Conspirators." Why does this matter? Falsifying a headline about the John Adams Project, exaggerating its importance, and obscuring its lack of clients makes it a deceptively impressive vehicle for an eight-figure fundraising campaign.

The ACLU's fundraising appeals were breathtakingly dishonest: "Make no mistake about it, when an ACLU legal team steps into the hearing room at Guantánamo Bay to defend detainees held there for years without charges, it will be a singularly important day for American freedom," a June 16, 2008, fundraising letter declared, falsely implying that the ACLU was taking the lead in representing Guantánamo detainees, and seeking "up to $15 million dollars" to do so. "The truth is, if the ACLU doesn't step forward and take on this work, no one else will." But the truth was, other organizations and individual attorneys had stepped forward years earlier to "take on this work," while the ACLU shirked it.

The Center for Constitutional Rights apparently noticed the omission of any mention of its work and instantly responded to the initial, April 4, 2008, announcement of the John Adams Project with an unusually piqued press release stressing its own six-year-long effort to provide representation to Guantánamo detainees: "I am pleased the ACLU and the National Association of Criminal Defense Lawyers are joining the Center for Constitutional Rights in challenging the Military Commissions at Guantánamo and trying to provide adequate counsel for men facing the death penalty based on evidence obtained though torture," CCR executive director Vince Warren (a former ACLU staff attorney) commented archly, adding that "the Center began the legal battle over Guantánamo in early 2002." Foundation officials who supported CCR's effort (and also supported the ACLU) were most likely aware of the essential fraudulence of the ACLU's new initiative, and, at least initially, the John Adams Project reportedly failed to obtain support from two major liberal funders, the Open Society Institute and Atlantic Philanthropies. The lack of support for Romero was unusual, as was CCR's implicit public rebuke of the ACLU. While, in private, a few civil liberties leaders and activists strongly criticized the ACLU's lobbying or litigation efforts or expressed misgivings about Romero's fitness for office, in public they remained silent or joined in a chorus of politic praise.

The ACLU pretended to lead while belatedly following, and interested onlookers as well as insiders generally pretended not to notice. The John Adams Project typified a pattern: with public relations driving policy more than an instinctive commitment to civil liberty, the ACLU avoids what appear to be financially risky or simply unrewarding civil liberties battles. When a battle is waged by others and proves lucrative, or when people notice that the ACLU is AWOL, it embarks on a PR campaign, effectively taking credit for others' victories and implying that it has been engaged in the struggle all along. Standing on the sidelines, jumping in front of the pack right before the finish line, the ACLU is becoming the Rosie Ruiz of advocacy groups.

II

Consider the ACLU's initial silence when the state of Texas raided a polygamous compound, the Yearning for Zion Ranch, and forcibly removed over four hundred children from their parents, on the basis of an anonymous phone call (an apparent hoax). The raid occurred on April 3, 2008, but the ACLU did not squeak up until April 18, when Judge Barbara Walther refused to release the children from state custody and ordered all parents and children to undergo mandatory DNA testing. The children were summarily detained on the basis of assumptions, not evidence of abuse, and the mandatory DNA testing appeared to be, at least in part, a post facto effort to obtain evidence justifying a blatantly illegal raid. But the ACLU, which generally opposes mandatory DNA testing of everyone arrested, much less detained in a spirit of protectiveness, offered only a cautious statement of "concern" about civil liberties and the "serious and difficult issues regarding the sometimes competing rights of children and their parents."[8]

This was a serious case, obviously, but difficult? From a civil libertarian perspective, identifying gross violations of individual rights by Texas law enforcement was easy. The state seized hundreds of children from their parents without bothering to show that they were abused or in danger of being abused, in clear, categorical violation of Texas law, as the Texas courts subsequently ruled.[9] Assumptions that all children were in danger were based partly on animus toward polygamists and partly on the reported discovery, after the raid, that twenty females were or had been pregnant before turning eighteen. But the fathers were unknown, and as the state later conceded, "teenage pregnancy, by itself, is not a legal basis for removing children from their home and parents."[10] (The state also seized toddlers and grade school children, who were not even alleged to be at risk of abuse.)

Even proof that some minors had been abused, however (which the state lacked), would not have proved that all minors on the ranch were at immediate risk. Imagine if the polygamist compound had instead been a community of Christian Scientists in which several children had become seriously ill after being treated only with prayer. It's highly unlikely that the state would have summarily seized all healthy children and placed them in foster care, without even trying to formulate a less drastic means of protecting them. Parents may be prosecuted for denying their children essential care for religious or nonreligious reasons, but the state does not and may not take preemptive action against Christian Scientists, based on a presumption that their children are at risk.

But while the legal analysis of the Texas raid was easy, the initial public relations challenge of opposing the raid was hard. Standing up for the rights of Mormon fundamentalists, generally derided as "weird" or "creepy" and presumed guilty of child abuse by liberals and conservatives alike, would have required courage of the ACLU and a willingness to take financial risks in defense of civil liberty. So, after remaining silent for two weeks, the Texas ACLU equivocated, in its April 18, 2008, press release:

> "While we acknowledge that Judge Walthers' task may be unprecedented in Texas judicial history, we question whether the current proceedings adequately protect the fundamental rights of the mothers and children of the FLDS," Terri Burke, executive director of the ACLU of Texas, remarked.

"As this situation continues to unfold, we are concerned that the constitutional rights that all Americans rely upon and cherish—that we are secure in our homes, that we may worship as we please and hold our places of worship sacred, and that we may be with our children absent evidence of imminent danger—have been threatened," Burke added.

This general acknowledgment that summarily removing hundreds of children threatened fundamental rights was barely preferable to the silence that preceded it. The ACLU's April 18 statement was an exercise in public relations; standing neither for nor against the state's unprecedented actions, it seemed designed to offend no one, while providing cover should the ACLU ever be accused of ducking a controversial civil liberties case. The statement carefully paid deference to the state power to protect children (ignoring the dearth of evidence of abuse and the failure to provide individualized hearings to Yearning for Zion families), and it carefully stressed that the ACLU "deplores crimes against children" and "stand[s] opposed to child abuse," in case anyone thought the ACLU stood in favor of it.

Anxious about appearing soft on child abuse, the ACLU apparently preferred being soft on civil liberties. The polygamous practices of Mormon fundamentalists are generally repugnant to ACLU supporters, particularly its feminist supporters, even if they don't involve the abuse of children. But hostility to Mormon polygamists is a reason for speaking up in defense of their rights, not an excuse for the ACLU's silence, obviously.

Hostility to polygamists does, however, provide an explanation for the ACLU's timidity in this case. If the polygamist compound had been a compound of allegedly illegal immigrants, the ACLU would, no doubt, have responded quickly and forcefully. Sympathy for illegal immigrants is strong within the ACLU, which considers immigrant rights a priority, featured prominently in its fundraising campaigns.

So when federal immigration authorities summarily rounded up immigrant workers in a surprise raid at a New Bedford factory in March 2007, the ACLU immediately entered the fray, defending the rights of workers and the estimated 210 children affected by the roundup of their parents, joining a lawsuit challenging federal abuses of power.[11] This was an important case, involving a humanitarian emergency and raising fundamental questions of due process—just like the raid on the Yearning for Zion compound.

Eventually, as hundreds of children from the compound were consigned to the notorious Texas foster-care system, as attorneys continued challenging the state's action and the media raised questions about it, the ACLU did finally speak up with a little conviction in defense of individual rights, in a May 2, 2008, statement, some four weeks after the raid.[12] Without venturing to accuse the state of constitutional violations, the ACLU expressed "serious concerns that the state's actions so far have not adequately protected the fundamental rights at stake," stressing that hundreds of children were removed absent individualized determinations of abuse and objecting to the mandatory DNA testing. The ACLU promised to "monitor the unfolding events . . . making our views known to the Texas courts at appropriate points in the judicial proceedings." In other words, the ACLU was prepared to submit a friend of the court brief in a case brought by one of the parties, which was the least it could do. Finally, an appellate court in Texas invalidated the state raid, and the ACLU submitted an amicus brief to the Texas Supreme Court, elaborating on the state's constitutional violations.[13] By the end of June, some two months after the raid, the ACLU was trumpeting its objections to the Texas raid on its home page, implying that it had long been in the forefront of this battle too.

I'd be surprised if many board members were cognizant of the ACLU's weak and dilatory defense of liberty in this case, but they quickly learned that the prominent Guantánamo initiative—the John Adams Project—was not what it initially appeared to be. At an April 2008 board meeting, only

a few weeks after the project was unveiled, Romero admitted that his "dream team" didn't actually represent anyone:
"[W]e need to line up the clients," the minutes record him acknowledging. According to one observer, most board members seemed unconcerned. Even when the emperor admitted
he was naked, the audience politely applauded his attire.

Months later, in November 2008, members reacted simi-
larly to news that Romero had funded the project with an un-
authorized transfer of $15 million from ACLU reserves. This
transfer was noticed not by the somnambulant board but
by *New York Times* reporter Stephanie Strom, whose inquiries about it (distributed to the board) elicited little apparent
concern about financial practices (with a few exceptions) but
some anger over her access to financial data. One member
protested that the ACLU's finances were confidential, forgetting perhaps that the ACLU is a public charity and that information Strom cited had been distributed at a public board
meeting. Executive committee member Roz Litman proposed
ferreting out Strom's sources. Newly elected president Susan
Herman referred her queries to an ACLU spokesperson who,
in a torrent of words, generally avoided responding to them.
When Strom pressed on, Herman noted in a November 11,
2008, e-mail to staff that Strom had "caught" them in an in-
consistency: "Is it best for me to continue not to respond to
her questions on this," or should they tell Strom the "real
answer," Herman asked; which response would be "worse for
her to report?" If the John Adams Project was primarily a
fundraising ploy, enabled by financial improprieties, it was
defended by staff and lay leaders with righteous disingenuousness. Some insiders disapproved of the ACLU's flummery
but also seemed stymied by it, if not resigned.

III

Institutionalized dishonesty is demoralizing. In a "totalitarian organization" devoted to maintaining and projecting its
own false image, "work, the productive process, becomes
display . . . and becomes mere ritual," Howard F. Schwartz

writes. "Realistic and concerned persons lose the belief that the organizations' real purpose is productive work and come to the conclusion that its real purpose is self-promotion."[14] At the ACLU, board members who recognized and recoiled from the increasing devotion to propaganda at the expense of performance tended either to retire or reduce the time and energy they devoted to the organization (if they were not voted off the board for making their concerns known). New board members, carefully vetted, tended to believe that the carefully cultivated images of the ACLU reflected reality; with little institutional knowledge and no history, they had little reason to believe otherwise. Staff members, focused more narrowly on particular administrative or programmatic responsibilities, could sometimes successfully ignore incremental institutional decay. Some staff members still engage in actual civil liberties work, for actual, not imaginary, clients, especially when their work serves the ACLU's public relations interests or, at least, doesn't conflict with them. But others have been deeply disenchanted by the ACLU's loss of integrity and have either found new jobs or were fired (sometimes with severance packages securing their silence), or they managed to hold on to their ACLU jobs and, at least, went through the motions of performing them—which was sometimes all that was required, or allowed.

"I saw my ability to do my job compromised because statements or recommendations I made in the context of my job responsibilities were being ignored and I was even warned not to make them," one former employee recalls. "That was compounded by what I saw happen to other long-time employees—I saw them increasingly demoralized and fired." This former staffer, who like all current and former employees critical of the Romero regime would speak only on condition of absolute anonymity, expected to remain at the ACLU until retirement: "You got to do work that you loved; your political life and your work life blended seamlessly. Then, things started to change around 2002. Something of the PR apparatus began to show through the communications efforts. More important for me, I lost faith that the organization was being true to its principles."

Employees who worried about the ACLU's departure from principle were divided from those who either accepted or denied it, another long-serving employee observed in a private e-mail to me a few years ago, describing a new culture at the ACLU "intolerant of disagreement, openness, and fairness":

> We now have a very serious divide at the ACLU. We have the haves and have nots. The have nots are employees who work in fear of arbitrary firing and retribution. They are generally old time employees who are committed to the organization's ideals. There are also a small number of new employees in the have not set. All these employees, old and new, have witnessed Anthony's inequities and breaches of principle first hand, and the board's tolerance of them, and they are deeply demoralized.
>
> The haves are employees who benefit from Anthony's largess in terms of immense and disproportionate salary increases in exchange for total devotion and obedience. Some are new employees and some are old employees who see what the have nots see but keep their heads down and cash their paychecks. They abandon their colleagues who are mistreated and are comfortable with the company line that only a few board critics are the problem, and are out to destroy Anthony and the organization for their own sick pleasure. In fact, they welcome the claims, which make it easier for them to look away when Anthony violates ACLU policies or acts unscrupulously. When asked questions about Anthony's conduct, they say he is not doing anything wrong. When asked if they know what he is doing, they say no.[15]

Thriving, not merely surviving, in an environment like this generally requires a capacity for self-deception or the

cheerful acknowledgment of your own complicity in deceiv-
ing others. Cynics and self-deceivers are favored by organizations that value image over performance, as Schwartz writes,
and both speed the organization's decay. "Cynicism tends
toward corruption . . . [although] cynics at least know what's
going on around them. . . . The more serious problem comes
in with those who deceive themselves and distance themselves from reality. . . . Since this capacity for self-deception
is an important advantage in the race for promotion, the to-
tal disassociation of the individual from organizational reality is likely to be correlated with the individuals' position in
the hierarchy. Then, the most important processes within the
organization come to be under the authority of people who
are not operating in the real world as far as the organization's
requirements are concerned."[16]

"When you're in the White House bubble, it's all consum-
ing," former Bush press secretary Scott McClellan observed
on *Meet the Press,* on June 1, 2008, rationalizing his participation in what he belatedly condemned as administration
propaganda campaigns. "I got caught up in the permanent
campaigns culture just like so many others do all too often in
today's poisonous Washington environment."

In other words, everybody does it, cynics and naifs alike,
and the naifs, at least, are victims of their "poisonous environments," or so McClellan implied. But environments don't
exist entirely independently of the people in them. Not quite
everybody does it: some quietly resist; a few loudly resign.
People choose to be "caught up" in a campaign culture; they
choose loyalty to a group over qualms about its character or
concerns about its effectiveness. They choose a moral code
that requires applauding playacting, instead of exposing or
critiquing it.

8

Gag Rules

I

How do you know when the virtues of association have devolved into vice? Loyalty to the institution prevails over
loyalty to the institution's ideals. The ACLU's ideals did not
long survive an assault on the idealized image of its leadership. After three years of internecine conflict and a series of
stories in the *New York Times* exposing the ACLU's apparent
hypocrisies, the executive committee and an ad hoc committee selected in 2005 by the president (rubber-stamped by the
board) chose to protect the institution from criticism instead
of protecting criticism from institutional authority.

On May 19, 2006, by a 9 to 1 vote and with the obvious
support of the leadership, a committee on "rights and responsibilities of board members" issued a final report including
these rules for board approval:

> "Where an individual director disagrees with a Board
> position on matters of civil liberties policy, the direc-
> tor should refrain from publicly highlighting the fact
> of such disagreement, particularly where the purpose
> or principal effect of such publicity is to call into
> question the integrity of the process in arriving at the
> Board's decision."

> "Directors should remember that there is always a
> material prospect that public airing of the disagree-

ment will affect the ACLU adversely in terms of public support and fundraising."

"[A] director may publicly disagree with an ACLU
policy position, but may not criticize the ACLU
Board or staff."

The proposed rules contradicted each other (as well as
settled policy guaranteeing free speech to ACLU boards and
staff). Directors were given permission to disagree publicly
with ACLU policy positions while also being admonished
to "refrain from publicly highlighting the fact of such disagreement." But putting aside the illogic of the recommendations, they made sense when you considered the nature of
the "disagreement" they aimed to suppress and the interests
they sought to protect. Public disagreements with policy positions were permissible, but strongly discouraged, if they
raised questions about institutional integrity—whether or
not the questions were merited. In other words, the proposed
rules implied, if the ACLU board acts without integrity, it
should be allowed to do so in relative secret. But in some
ways this caveat was merely redundant, since directors were
strongly discouraged from ever airing their disagreements
with ACLU policy so as not to "adversely" affect fundraising.
    The unself-conscious hypocrisy of these proposals
was a disturbing indication of the board's increasing, self-
defeating irrationalism. The ACLU leadership and many
board members were obsessed with protecting the ACLU's
image, even at the expense of its ideals, and lacked any sense
of how much they damaged the image by jettisoning the ideals. The ACLU urged other institutions, public and private,
to protect free speech, regardless of how deeply it insulted
people or how much it cost, but within the ACLU, free speech
would be suppressed, or strongly discouraged, because its
potential costs to fundraising and reputation were deemed
prohibitive.
    Equally revealing and even more absurd was the provi-

sion distinguishing between disagreement and criticism, explicitly allowing public disagreement with an ACLU policy position, while prohibiting criticism of the board or staff. At the very least, this ban on criticism reflected a lack of imagination: to appreciate its flaws, you had only to wonder how the ACLU might react to a law permitting us to disagree with government policy but prohibiting criticism of government officials. In endorsing this rule, the rights and responsibilities committee and the leadership were endorsing an ACLU sedition act.

The endorsement was not accidental, but I doubt it was supposed to be so obvious. The allowance for "disagreement" seemed intended to provide rhetorical cover; its transparency reflected the insularity of the people who drafted and approved it, with apparent misplaced confidence that it was opaque. The distinction between disagreement and criticism was obviously semantic: when you disagree with a policy, you implicitly criticize the judgment of people who adopted it. When you ban criticism, you ban dissent.

Only a few weeks before we received this policy, Romero himself had demonstrated how easily disagreement could be equated with criticism when he loudly denounced me at a board meeting for "attacking" an ACLU staff member by expressing disagreement with an ACLU policy. I had publicly dissented from the ACLU's endorsement of a bill barring antiabortion "crisis counseling" centers from advertising "abortion services," making no references to any ACLU staff or board members.[1] But at a subsequent April 2006 board meeting, Romero interrupted a debate about the bill by launching into a tirade against me for "attacking" a member of his staff, whom he claimed to be defending. (In fact, by defending a staffer I hadn't mentioned from an attack I hadn't made, Romero slyly implied that she was to blame for supporting the controversial bill.)

This performance had unintended consequences; it elicited criticism from other board members, and a review of it appeared in the *New York Times*, along with an account of its epilogue. Immediately after yelling at me, Romero turned to board member Alison Steiner, who had been visibly upset by his tirade, and summoned her out of the room; then, according to her report (which was quoted in the *Times*), he chastised her for appearing upset while he was assailing me. "Anthony went on to say that because I was Wendy's 'friend' and did not appear ready to join him in 'getting rid of her,' (by, among other things, lobbying her affiliate to remove her as its representative) I was no better than she was, and then stormed off angrily," Steiner wrote in an e-mail to the board. "Later in the meeting," as the *Times* reported, "Mr. Romero asked another board member, David F. Kennison, to step outside after Mr. Kennison apologized for failing to object to Mr. Romero's attack on Ms. Kaminer." In his report to the board, Kennison described his encounter with Romero: "He told me that he would 'never' apologize to [Kaminer] and that his evaluation of her performance as a member of this board was justified by information he had been accumulating in a 'thick file on her.'"[2]

But embarrassing publicity like this only intensified the board's support for Romero and anger at his critics, and his attack on me served his purpose. It dramatized the risk of disagreeing publicly with an ACLU policy position: being singled out and publicly castigated by the leader of the pack—a risk most members instinctively avoid. Looking back, I don't think Romero's outburst was spontaneous (in any case, Strossen seemed unsurprised by it). I think it was, in part, calculated to intimidate other incipient critics and chill dissent, even from ACLU positions on civil liberties, which had always been subject to public debate. I think it was a prelude to the fiduciary rights and responsibilities proposal banning criticism of the ACLU, which Romero knew we were about to receive.

That proposal was circulated to the board a few weeks later, on May 19, 2006, in a final report from the rights and responsibilities committee; it was also sent, or "leaked," to Stephanie Strom at the *New York Times* and was the subject of a May 24 article (the same article that described Romero's performance at the April 2006 board meeting). Naturally, the ACLU leadership and its supporters throughout the organization reacted furiously to this latest "leak," but the no-dissent proposal, soon to be discussed at a public meeting, disclosed no confidential information; it was simply a proposed code of conduct for board members. In fact, people who fulminated about the leak to the press also expressed incomprehension that the *Times* deemed an ACLU proposal banning dissent at all newsworthy: "I would expect to see this kind of 'news' in the tabloids, not the NY Times!" a member of the committee that proposed the new gag rule declared in an e-mail to the board. He later stressed, "There [was] nothing inherently controversial about the guidelines we propose," which might make you wonder why he worried about their public exposure. Another board member complained in a letter he sent to the *Times* (and shared with the board) that the article was "part of an ongoing vendetta in which a few unhappy present and former board members display dirty laundry to a got-ya journalist in return for national publicity." He added that the proposal described in the article was a "draft of standards for board members percolating deep within a committee that hasn't even been circulated to the board."

The insistence that this embarrassing proposal was a confidential, not yet circulated draft was false: it was a final committee report, the product of some eighteen months of deliberation; it had been reviewed by the leadership months earlier and distributed electronically to the board days before the *Times* article appeared. But once exposed, the proposal naturally aroused the consternation of donors and members and generated editorials ridiculing the ACLU for failing to practice what it so loudly preached. Naturally, advocates of this allegedly uncontroversial, unnewsworthy effort to ban dissent vainly sought to distance themselves from it, and the verifiably false description of the proposal as a preliminary, confidential draft was repeated with suspicious regularity by board members and staff in comments to affiliate boards and to the press. I'd bet my yearly ACLU contribution that it was an official "talking point" widely distributed by the national office: "The proposal regarding rights and responsibilities of national Board members apparently is in a draft stage and has not yet been reviewed by national staff or discussed by the national Board," one affiliate executive director dutifully reported to her board. (I imagine she offered similar assurances to concerned donors.) "Ms. Strom quotes out of context from the working draft of unfinished committee recommendations that the vast majority of ACLU board and executive committee members have never seen," a member of the executive committee wrongly stated in an e-mail to his state affiliate board. In fact, the executive committee on which he served had reviewed the recommendations at least once, five months earlier.

The rights and responsibilities committee report was distributed at a January 6, 2006, executive committee meeting and briefly discussed, in a taped conversation. Romero can be heard on tape commenting on the report; Rob Remar pronounced it "excellent" and no one, including Nadine Strossen or Romero, disagreed or expressed any qualms about banning dissent. Romero also had no apparent qualms about subsequently denying that he had seen, much less discussed, this proposed ban. He "said he had not yet read the proposals," the *Times* reported;[3] he "hadn't even had the chance to review it," Romero wrote in an e-mail to the national board, the day before the *Times* article appeared.

Am I nitpicking once again? Were these false denials excusable or of little import? Individually, they were easily overlooked. Collectively, however, they obscured important truths about the loss of integrity, or maybe sanity, at the ACLU. But the board had become accustomed to the face-saving statements routinely circulated to the press and throughout the organization (with the aid of many board members) in response to the periodic exposure of "mistakes."

This entrenched tolerance for official falsities suggested

tacit agreement that boards have a fiduciary duty to lie or acquiesce in the dissemination of lies when a potentially costly truth is rationalized as trivial, irrelevant, or subordinate to an organizational mission. Or, as board members were apt to observe, more sympathetically, we should always "put a positive spin on things," especially when talking to the media. Objecting to "positive spin" or public relations seems petty or simply naive, and some truths are trivial, but then, so are the consequences of acknowledging them. Fibbing is most excusable when it's least necessary. At the ACLU, it became essential.

Concealing the truth was rationalized by the usual assertion that concealment served a greater good. Consider, again, the proposed rule admonishing directors to "refrain from publicly highlighting" disagreements that "call into question" the "integrity" of board processes—a rule making no exception for cases in which the questions were valid and apt to be ignored internally. No group is likely to respond with any integrity to a charge of diminished integrity that happens to be true, obviously; the no-dissent proposal implicitly assumed that ethical charges against the ACLU would always be false, or petty, like a compendium of minor mistakes.

The proposal was expressly designed to deter and punish exposure of such mistakes, even to ACLU members; it defined confidential "proprietary" information broadly, for example, to include any "information about internal organizational stewardship (*e.g.,* staffing, fundraising, resource allocation)." This might be a reasonable rule in another organization, but it violated the ACLU's tradition of transparency, as well as its open-meetings policy: how could discussions held at public meetings be considered confidential? And given the new primacy of fundraising at the ACLU, a rule that prohibited airing any information about fundraising would have prohibited the airing of important civil liberties issues: had this rule been in effect in 2004, directors would have been barred from discussing with ACLU supporters the debate about private grants restrictions on speech or the ACLU's approval of the Combined Federal Campaign watch-list agreement.

Questions about the rights of members and donors to know embarrassing truths about the organization they supported were not asked during our battles about leaking and lying, but they were effectively answered: lies told to the press were lies told to ACLU supporters. Indeed, members and donors were primary targets of official misinformation, as well as the primary audience for leaks. But the ethical code reflected in the no-dissent proposal, and the board's underlying willingness to tolerate apparent misconduct preferred lying to the press over leaking to the press, regarding lies as morally necessary responses to leaks. This was not an academic moral choice: it enabled violations of fundamental civil liberties principles, as well as cover-ups of lapses in governance. It relieved Romero, Strossen, and other board leaders of the need to lie convincingly, without contradicting themselves or each other. A majority of people who had reason to know the truth had implicitly acknowledged the moral necessity of concealing it. Internally, the leadership enjoyed implausible deniability.

But reality intruded when their shenanigans were revealed externally, in the press. The no-dissent proposal could not survive its public ridicule, and the leadership planned a retreat: Romero invited *Times* reporter Stephanie Strom to the June 2006 board meeting, apparently intending to disavow the proposal publicly (although in response to a question, he mistakenly launched into a speech against it prematurely, before it was on the floor and before she arrived). Still, a mere six state affiliates had submitted resolutions opposing the proposed gag rule; the rights and responsibilities committee defended it (with the exception of lone dissenter Alison Steiner), and during a two-hour discussion only a small minority of board members clearly objected to it; about an equal number supported it. The *Times* report on this meeting apparently generated another wave of protest from donors, and Strossen soon announced abruptly that the ban on dissent was being withdrawn.

It had never been necessary. Dissent had been silenced informally by ostracizing, deriding, and vilifying dissenters, encouraging them to resign or defeating them electorally, and denying the truth of their claims, however absurdly. As Susan Herman advised at a February 2006 executive committee meeting, "peer group pressure" could promote "responsible dissent," discouraging "freelancing" that disregarded "what the majority of the board thinks." No one responded to this little Orwellianism by pointing out the obvious: dissent *means* opposition to "what the majority thinks." Suggesting that responsible dissenters should defer to the majority is like suggesting that protesters should not express disagreement. Herman also criticized the "radical individualism" of the ACLU's unnamed, irresponsible dissenters, and no one reminded her that radical individualism was precisely what civil libertarians were supposed to value and protect. Imagine a world without radical individualists and you imagine a world without dissenters; you imagine the new ACLU.

With no apparent sense of irony or self-awareness, ACLU leaders had abandoned the fundamental commitment to protecting minority rights and minority views from majority rule. They had righteously succumbed to the prerogatives of power, persuading or intimidating a board majority into conceding that they were doing so not out of self-interest but in the interests of the ACLU. They erred strategically in promoting a no-dissent rule partly because they failed to appreciate their own success. As one longtime board member observed at the June 2006 board meeting, objecting to the stated ban on dissent, "Words like this . . . shouldn't exist on paper at all." At the ACLU, as in other liberal groups and communities, the most effective bans on dissent are the most insidious; unspoken, they leave no trace but silence.

II

None dare call it censorship. Liberal advocates of banning "hate speech" or other forms of incivility tend to regard censorship as a conservative vice, despite their own embrace of it. They assert their respect for free speech by defining it narrowly: "Free speech doesn't include hate speech" or the right to "offend," they insist nonsensically—as if we'd need free speech guarantees to protect the right not to offend. Restraints on speech are also cloaked in the therapeutic rhetoric of tolerance, sensitivity, psychic safety, or civility. Appropriately, perhaps, the liberal romance with censorship is a love that dare not speak its name.*

ACLU leaders were naturally loath to admit their support for restricting board members' speech; even as they sought the enactment of an official gag rule, they claimed to be promoting civility, not censorship. While the rule was designed to silence the leadership's internal critics (and would probably never have been proposed had the board been at peace), its consistency with fashionable liberal notions of censorship was not exactly coincidental. Board members are almost uniformly liberal or progressive politically, and their concerns about civil liberty are often qualified by a commitment to diversity that's sometimes hostile to free speech. The ideologies that helped rationalize the internal no-dissent proposal, providing the rhetoric that defended it, also demanded an increasingly selective approach to defending dissent externally (which I'll examine). Liberal censorship, tolerated and (in recent years) occasionally advanced by the ACLU is not exactly an associational vice (or at least not a readily recognizable one), but it is a form of collectivism blind to individualism's virtues. The ACLU's creeping authoritarianism in the midst of internecine conflict should also be viewed in the larger context of liberalism's declining commitment to liberty, which, for years, has manifested itself most clearly and, regrettably, most effectively on college campuses.

Since censorship is apt to be most successful when it proceeds euphemistically, liberal or progressive campus censors

---

*By focusing on left-wing censorship, I don't mean to minimize or excuse right-wing censorship. It is simply not my subject.

typically pledge their allegiance to free speech right before offering justifications for restricting it. Take the Vassar College code on "academic freedom and responsibility": "Vassar College is dedicated to freedom of inquiry in the pursuit of truth, and is vigilant in defending the right of individuals to free speech," the code proclaims. The "but" immediately follows: "The college, however, is also a community dedicated to the cultivation of an atmosphere in which all of its members may live and work free from intolerance, disrespect, or harassment."[4]

There's the rub. Your freedom of speech ends where my sensibilities begin. Vassar's policy subtly indicates that the college will not honor the constitutional ideal of free speech, by stressing its status as a private institution exempt from the obligation to respect First Amendment rights and entitled to establish its own rules governing speech and behavior. Students are not likely to recognize this as a disavowal of First Amendment guarantees, but lawyers will: "Vassar is a voluntary association of persons invited to membership on the understanding that they will respect the principles by which it is governed."

Those principles elevate the perceived demands of a demographically diverse community over freedom of speech: "Vassar is a residential college, and because it seeks diversity in its membership, individuals have a particular obligation beyond that of society at large to exercise self-restraint, tolerance for difference, and regard for the rights and sensitivities of others." In other words, the Vassar administration is not obliged to refrain from censoring whatever it deems intolerant or insensitive speech; instead members of the Vassar community are obliged to refrain from engaging in it.

Repression of individual rights is justified as a force for collective liberation: "Genuine freedom of mind is not possible in the absence of civility," Vassar's statement on freedom and responsibility asserts, with autocratic illogic. "Freedom is about authority," former New York mayor and 2008 presidential candidate Rudy Giuliani proclaimed, echoing

Vassar's creed. "Freedom is about the willingness of every single human being to cede to lawful authority a great deal of discretion about what you do."[5] In an age of political correctness, authoritarianism is where right and left meet.

Conservative and liberal censors alike target whatever speech derides or offends their respective constituent groups. Giuliani famously tried retaliating against the Brooklyn Museum for an art exhibit that offended Catholics. Liberal colleges take aim at speech that denigrates affirmative action or orthodoxies of identity politics. At Vassar, in 2005, a conservative student magazine, the *Imperialist,* was punished for publishing an anonymous column critiquing separatism—the tendency of students to divide themselves by race, ethnicity, and sexual orientation. Vassar's professed dedication to "free inquiry" did not include the freedom to say this: "How is diversity achieved when students are voluntarily confining themselves to ghettos of the ALANA [African, Latino, Asian and Native American] Center and Blegen House [a "resource center for Lesbian, Gay, Bisexual, Transgender, and Queer communities"]? I find the objective of diversity to be utterly meritless, suggesting that our colleges should become some zoological preserve in some paternalistic attempt [to] benefit our 'non diverse' students." You can call this passage inelegant, but off campus, you'd be hard pressed to place it outside the realm of civil discourse (never mind the right to be uncivil). On campus, however, some students were predictably infuriated by this column and by a cartoon showing a black student intimidating a white student by calling her a racist. As a result, the *Imperialist* lost funding and suspended publication for a year. Vassar proved itself vigilant in policing, not protecting, speech.[6]

It's worth noting that the target of the *Imperialist*'s critique—identity politics—was also the reason for its punishment: the magazine was essentially charged and convicted of group libel (or its equivalent on American campuses) for offending members of the usual protected groups. When free speech is dismissed as a mere instrument of power, not a basic human right, when it is perversely associated with the oppression of historically victimized groups, and not their liberation, censorship is deemed a liberating act of self-defense, dedicated to achieving collective equality.

The righteous tribalism of identity politics creates virtual associations—of racial and ethnic minorities, women, and gay, disabled, or overweight people, among other presumptively victimized groups. Students can identify with several groups simultaneously, which may complicate but also intensifies interest in belonging and enjoying the multiple benefits of multiple memberships, including the rights as well as the deference afforded protected classes. Identity politics encourages people to regard themselves as members of their groups first and individuals second and to locate free speech rights, or the lack of them, in group demands for respect, not in the claims of individual conscience. Morality is then on the side of censoring "offensive" speech, not indulging in it; dissent that challenges the ideology of identity is condemned as a form of bigotry, or disloyalty if it comes from within: if I seek to protect speech considered sexist and harmful to women, then, in the view of some feminists, I am a traitor to my sex—the virtual association of women.

This is, by now, an old story of therapeutic politics. In the late 1980s and early '90s the convergence of the antiporn movement with multiculturalism and expansive, popular therapeutic notions of abuse helped obliterate the distinction between words and action, equating the harm of insults or "verbal abuse" with the harm of actual assaults. The therapeutic sanctification of personal testimony (reflected in the popularity of memoirs) legitimized subjective definitions of abusive speech. One individual's interest in speaking her mind is righteously subordinated to another's demand for comfort or respect (as she defines it) based on her membership in a recognized identity group. Censorship and ideological coercion are rationalized (and renamed—as civility or mutual respect and inclusiveness) in pursuit of diverse communities in which all members can feel "safe"—so long as they practice safe speech.

"There is no parity between the feeling of a person for

his own opinion and the feeling of another who is offended
at his holding it, no more than the desire of a thief to take
a purse and the desire of the right owner to keep it," John
Stuart Mill observed.[7] But if Mill is still read, he is often ignored. On hundreds of campuses, vague, overbroad civility,
harassment, and speech codes and various forms of sensitivity training typically give administrators virtually un-
bridled discretion to punish whatever speech and stigmatize
whatever ideas they deem offensive. "On campus, if you're
offended, if you're angry, if there's something you're just uncomfortable with, if there's an opinion you dislike, or if an
op-ed comes out that you disagree with, there's an all-too-
common tendency to call that harassment, and it happens
in case after case, after case," Greg Lukianoff, president of
the Foundation for Individual Rights in Education (FIRE)
laments.[8] (FIRE's mission is preserving civil liberties on
campus; I serve on its advisory board.) Humor and satire are
frequent targets of campus censors who punish students for
uttering the sort of jokes they hear regularly on *South Park* or
The Daily Show.[9]

Political correctness has been the subject of ridicule
and outrage for years, but it continues to worsen. The group
inequalities that liberal censorship is designed to address
are increasingly, absurdly minute, especially on campus: students are encouraged to turn ordinary slights of everyday
life into melodramas of oppression. "They're Sitting Right
Next to Us," a headline in the *Boston Globe* shrieks, in a remarkably unbalanced, 2007 story on "ethnic tensions and
racist attitudes" that might have been written by a midlevel
administrator defending a repressive speech code, or a recent
graduate weaned on one.[10]

What qualifies as "racism?" It includes "microaggressions" that are troubling precisely because they are "difficult
to report," as if people should be reported for giving offense.
The *Globe* approvingly cites a Boston College junior reporting that she often hears her fellow students exclaiming that
the ethnic food she and her friends eat in their rooms "smells
so bad," adding that remarks like these are troubling pre-

cisely because people can't be punished for making them. "You can't call the police and say, 'They're complaining about [my] food.' That's why it's so dangerous—there's no legal recourse."

It's tempting to view this complaint as anomalous, but the respect it was accorded by the *Boston Globe* is a measure of its normality, at least among many liberals. In fact, the *Globe* reporter may have exaggerated the student's concerns. She subsequently told me that she had been "grossly misquoted" and that her remarks were taken out of context, most misleadingly: "I was speaking about an incident that later led to a hate crime, lead pipes used as weapons, serious violence, and a student being expelled from the university," the student stated in an e-mail, months after the article appeared. But whether or not her remarks were accurately reported, they testify to a belief (by reporter Vanessa Jones, if not the young woman she interviewed) that students may be endangered by casual insults to their food and ought to have some "legal recourse" for them. Jones doesn't wonder how college students came to feel so fragile, so incapable of independently addressing or simply sloughing off the normal frictions of communal living, so averse to fighting their own, everyday battles without the assistance of paternalistic administrators.

Offering anecdotal evidence of presumed bigotry on campus (including criticisms of affirmative action or ethnic food), she doesn't question the belief that expressions of perceived bias should be actionable and that opposition to political correctness reflects opposition to equality. She approvingly quotes Simmons College assistant professor Daren Graves, who characterizes protests of PC as a backlash to the civil rights movement. "The people in power think things are moving too quickly," Graves opines. "What you might be seeing on campus is a reflection of what you're seeing in society in general: 'Let's slow down with this PC stuff. It's taking people out of their comfort zones. I have to watch my words and that's not what America's about.'"

Civil libertarians have good reason to worry about the

future when an assistant professor at a respected college so blithely dismisses the claim that America is not about suppressing speech (and a reporter for a major liberal newspaper repeats it uncritically). Graves needs to take, not teach, an elementary civics course, as well as classes in history and logic. "People in power" are apt to be the enemies, not the friends of free speech. Who does Graves imagine suppresses dissent—people without power? Does he think that campus speech codes reflect the powerlessness of campus officials who promulgate them or the students who invoke them as protection from offense?

At Tufts University, students are empowered to police each other. Freshman orientation includes "a group exercise that unveils bias," the *Globe* reports. A Bias Education Awareness Team "creates programming around bigotry and guides students on how to report bias incidents." Incidents may be reported and accessed online. "It's the everyday incidents that go unnoticed and unreported," one student explains, lauding the effort to create a network of informers that encourages people to watch what they say, and within whose earshot they say it.

If the causes of campus censorship are trivial—insults, opinions, and "microaggressions"—the consequences are not. Students taught to censor themselves and to expect others to be punished for offending them will be ill-equipped to participate in the uncivil arenas of democracy and social change, where we do not and should not have a right not to be insulted or upset. Your right to speak is no right at all if it's contingent on my emotional fortitude. Essential, controversial political speech is often profoundly upsetting, as the emotionalism of protests and counterprotests shows. Reproductive-choice advocates complain that women seeking abortions can be traumatized by protests outside abortion clinics. The survivors of soldiers killed in Iraq can be greatly pained by antiwar protests. In a free society we don't have a right to be protected from the emotional turmoil occasioned by speech; we do have a right to inflict it. This may seem hard-hearted, but liberty requires us to be hardheaded.

Or, you might argue that the preservation of liberty reflects a soft spot for individual integrity. The right to dissent has normative as well as instrumental value; it is a fundamental human right, essential to the preservation of individual integrity as well as liberty. Free speech advocates tend to oppose censorship primarily on instrumental grounds, stressing that it will lead us down the slippery slope of indiscriminately restricting "good" and "bad" speech alike. That's true, but if the practical threats of censorship could somehow be minimized or even eliminated, it would remain a violation of what should be the inalienable, moral right to speak and think freely. "We can never be sure that the opinion we are endeavoring to stifle is a false opinion; and if we were sure stifling it would be an evil still," Mill wrote.[11] I don't entirely agree that we can never be sure, or at least sure enough, about the falsity of an opinion; but I am certain that suppressing opinions is wrong. Censorship is suffocation, whether it reflects the establishment of collective identity groups that censorious liberals endorse or the dictates of custom that Mill decried.

You might expect the practical and moral threats of liberal censorship to be a great concern to the ACLU, but it often avoids intervening in campus speech wars, or responds to campus censorship with excessively cautious expressions of concern. When Brandeis University professor Donald Hindley was secretly investigated and found guilty of racial harassment for uttering the word "wetback" in the course of describing its use, the ACLU of Massachusetts issued a press release (on January 25, 2008) condemning racist speech, despite evidence that Hindley hadn't uttered any, and criticizing Brandeis not for censorship but for its failure to accord Hindley due process.

Historically, the Massachusetts ACLU has vigorously defended free speech, but these days it's part of a regime in which an ACLU employee could perhaps be chastised for innocently uttering the word "wetback," too: a 2005 "best practices" employee handbook for affiliates includes in its definition of harassment, "degrading . . . word[s] . . . toward . . . an individual's race, color, religion, sex, sexual orientation, age, [or] national origin." Sexual harassment is defined vaguely, subjectively (and elaborately) to include: "Conduct of any kind that is perceived to be sexual harassment by a supervisor or employee . . . the development of a perceived flirtatious personal relationship between two employees where one employee is in a position to assign or review the work of the other . . . the display in the work place of sexually suggestive objects or pictures, including nude photographs."

A prohibition of all nude photographs and any other "sexually suggestive" objects reflects a "procensorship . . . equation of sexual expression and sexual harassment" that former ACLU president Nadine Strossen sharply criticized in her 1995 book, *Defending Pornography.* There, Strossen lamented, "[a] growing body of sexual harassment rules are expressly barring much, if not all, sexual expression from workplaces and campuses." She expressed contempt for the "current epidemic of erotophobia" and outrage at policies restricting sexual expression on the basis of "subjective perceptions."[12] That was then. Strossen was president of the ACLU when it advised banning "perceived" sexual expression in the workplace, with at least her tacit support; she was president of the ACLU in 2006, when the policy was discussed on the national board Listserv. If Strossen had any objections to it, she did not share them with the board.

As the ACLU "best practices" antiharassment policy (and Strossen's 1995 book) indicates, identity politics and an accompanying belief in policing speech and ideologies offensive to particular groups are not unique to academia; overbroad workplace harassment codes recommended by risk-averse lawyers greatly restrict speech, in the interests of avoiding lawsuits. Speech policing flourishes in private institutions partly because managers unrestrained by the First

Amendment have the power to indulge in it. In 1995, Strossen argued that private sector employers and campus administrators "should respect free expression," nonetheless.[13] In 2006, she remained silent while the ACLU model antiharassment policy was described as an unfortunate necessity by the few board members who expressed concerns about its restrictions on speech. Yet the actual necessity of such a policy was unclear. Had the ACLU ever been sued by employees objecting to nude photographs in the workplace? Would it be taking an unreasonable risk if it did not prohibit the "development of a perceived flirtatious personal relationship" (whatever that means) between a supervisor and supervisee? Questions like these weren't raised during the board's brief electronic discussion of the policy, the necessity of which was assumed. Employers "probably have to listen to the experts and do what they suggest," one board member advised, rejecting the proposition that the ACLU should challenge laws and policies that infringe on speech, not perpetuate them.

The collective shrug that greeted this antilibertarian harassment policy reflected ideological changes that accelerated during Romero's tenure, as well as practical concerns about avoiding lawsuits. The ACLU was increasingly sympathetic to restrictions on speech promulgated in the interests of diversity and the protection of presumptively vulnerable groups: when the New York City Council enacted a "symbolic moratorium" on use of the word "nigger," in 2007, the New York Civil Liberties Union shrugged. "The Council is entitled to a point of view. It would be an entirely different matter if the Council was considering a law to ban the use of the n-word," the NYCLU executive director explained to the *New York Times*, ignoring the natural tendency of an official, symbolic ban on speech to legitimize an actual ban.[14] If the City Council passed a symbolic resolution denouncing flag burning or criticizing the president, I don't doubt that the NYCLU would oppose it vociferously. Ten years ago, I expect that it would have opposed an official moratorium on a racial epithet too, but by 2007, the culture of the ACLU had changed, as a direct result of new leadership and, indirectly, in response to progressive political culture and a belief that ensuring equality sometimes requires restricting free speech.

A commitment to equality is hardly new to the ACLU, which fought for racial equality in its early years, and again with renewed vigor in the mid 1960s, when racial injustice became and remained central to the ACLU's mission. For several decades, in the late twentieth century, it worked for civil rights without compromising its commitment to civil liberty. But by the 1990s, multiculturalism, the complexities of affirmative action aimed less at remedying past discrimination than ensuring future diversity, and the "progressive" notion that equality for presumptively vulnerable groups required protection from hateful or harassing speech posed inevitable challenges to the ACLU; its commitment to liberty and equality became increasingly difficult to reconcile. The conflicts were interesting and not necessarily unproductive; tensions between its right and left wings sometimes resulted in more nuanced policy positions. But after 9/11, the ACLU lost its balance, becoming markedly more liberal and less civil libertarian (except when civil liberties advocacy—like protests of Bush administration abuses—also served a liberal agenda).

The ACLU began describing itself as a "social justice organization," and its nonpartisan commitment to civil liberty shrank—especially its commitment to free speech—while its vision of equality expanded, even as it protested particular, post-9/11 threats to liberty. It became fashionably sensitive to incivility (as the NYCLU's tolerance for a "n-word" moratorium suggests), and began surrendering to identity politics, evidenced by new affirmative action requirements limiting board terms for nondisabled, heterosexual white males, mandating board membership goals for racial and ethnic minorities, women, disabled people, and gay, lesbian, bisexual, or transgendered people, and encouraging us to "self-identify" as members of one or more of these groups. It became selective in its defense of liberty, ignoring state action that trampled the fundamental rights of groups it disdained, as its instinctively tepid response to the blatantly unlawful raid on the Texas polygamist compound or its recent, relative passivity in defending the rights of antiabortion protesters showed. In 2007, Massachusetts barred even silent, peaceful protests within thirty-five feet of abortion clinics; the Massachusetts ACLU officially opposed the new buffer zone and spoke against it in the press but reportedly spent little capital trying to stop it in the legislature. The conservative Alliance Defense Fund mounted a challenge to it in federal court.[15]

The confluence of these trends is worth noting: the rise of liberal identity politics within the ACLU, the internal suppression of board dissent and employee speech rights, and a decreasing commitment to protecting politically incorrect speech outside the ACLU.

The ACLU's declining commitment to free speech is unacknowledged and not readily apparent, because it is obscured by deceptive public relations campaigns and because so much evidence of it lies in cases the ACLU does not take. It's naturally easier to know what an organization *is* doing (and advertising) than what it is not doing. But a review of recent free-speech press releases turns up disproportionately few cases in which ACLU state affiliates defended the rights of conservative, politically incorrect speakers. And in the past few years, the national organization has been remarkably quiet in several important free speech cases and controversies.

The ACLU was inexcusably, hypocritically absent from a very important 2006 student speech case, *Harper v. Poway*.[16] Harper involved a high school student's right to wear a T-shirt condemning homosexuality. Of course, the ACLU doesn't speak out on every case, but historically it has vigorously defended student speech rights, as its Web site stresses. In fact, while it avoided intervening in the *Harper* case, the ACLU was boasting of its representation of a student in a no more compelling free speech case, *Morse v. Frederick,* involving the right of a student to carry a nonsensical BONG HITS 4 JESUS banner at an off-campus event.[17] The ACLU pays particular attention to the right to wear T-shirts with pro-gay messages in school, proudly citing cases in which it represented students wearing pro-gay (as well as anti-Bush) T-shirts. In 2007, the ACLU awarded a Youth Activist Scholarship to a student who fought the efforts of her school to bar students from wearing T-shirts that said GAY, FINE BY ME.[18]

So in 2004, when Tyler Chase Harper was disciplined for wearing a T-shirt declaring his religious objections to homosexuality, civil libertarians might have expected the ACLU to protest loudly. (The front of his T-shirt declared, BE ASHAMED, OUR SCHOOL EMBRACED WHAT GOD HAS CONDEMNED; the back, HOMOSEXUALITY IS SHAMEFUL.) Harper was barred from attending classes when he wore this message to school on an official "Day of Silence," when gay students taped their mouths to symbolize the silencing effect of intolerance. Represented by the Alliance Defense Fund, he sued the school district. Less than a year later, the ACLU sued a Missouri school that barred a student from wearing "gay supportive T-shirts," eventually securing a promise from the school to "stop censoring," the ACLU Web site boasts.[19] Harper, however, was unsuccessful in his quest to stop school censorship. In a patronizing, antilibertarian decision in which Judge Stephen Reinhardt opted to protect the imagined feelings of gay students from the message on Harper's shirt, the Ninth Circuit rejected his First Amendment claims. (There was a sharp dissent from Judge Alex Kozinski.)[20]

Perhaps the ACLU was observing its own prolonged day of silence, because, while it pays close attention to federal appellate court decisions on civil liberties, it ignored this terrible precedent, even when Harper appealed to the Supreme Court. The Court dismissed the case as moot because Harper had graduated, but took the unusual step of vacating the decision so that it no longer exists as precedent (no thanks to the ACLU). Harper's younger sister, still in school, continued pressing his claims and, finally, after its silence in the *Harper* case was publicly criticized, the ACLU filed an amicus brief in her case.[21]

Tyler Harper had a particularly strong case, because in violating his speech rights, school officials also violated his right to the free exercise of religion. But despite its professed commitment to religious liberty, the ACLU is generally slow to defend the First Amendment rights of antigay, religious conservatives. As a staff member has privately acknowledged, it purposefully absents itself from cases on college campuses involving the associational rights of Christian student groups to discriminate against gay students, in accordance with their religious beliefs. But in some cases, conservative students might be grateful for the ACLU's silence: in an ultimately successful 2006 federal court challenge to an unconstitutional speech code at Georgia Tech, brought by the Alliance Defense Fund on behalf of conservative religious students, the ACLU filed a friend of the court brief ("in support of neither party") proposing adoption of an alternative "anti-harassment" code that included a prohibition on "injurious written/verbal communications . . . directed toward an individual because of their characteristics or beliefs."[22] In other words, the Georgia ACLU proposed punishing students for sharply criticizing or satirizing each other's beliefs if their remarks were deemed "injurious." Of course, the ACLU does sometimes defend the right to engage in antigay or otherwise "injurious" speech: the Ohio ACLU opposed legislation prohibiting protests near funerals, aimed at silencing the notorious Fred Phelps, who ranted and railed against homosexuality at military funerals. Following the lead of other free speech advocates, the Pennsylvania affiliate at least lent its name to a friend of the court brief opposing Temple University's overbroad harassment code, which was successfully challenged in federal court.[23] But the ACLU no longer defends the rights of "injurious" speakers consistently, with the courage of conviction.

Instead, as its silence in the *Harper* case testified, the

ACLU now operates under the influence of an antilibertarian, content-based approach to protecting speech that inevitably justifies censorship: "Take hate speech," Romero remarked to the *New York Times* in May 2006. "While believing in free speech, we do not believe in or condone speech that attacks minorities."[23] (Romero was responding to queries about the proposal to bar board members from criticizing the ACLU.)

He subsequently disavowed this remark, but the ACLU's actions, or inactions, have demonstrated the sad truth of it. In 2008, despite its new focus on international human rights, the ACLU declined to join a free speech coalition opposing a UN defamation of religion resolution that targeted criticism of Islam. Two years earlier, the ACLU had remained silent when Muslim groups violently protested publication of the Muhammad cartoons in the Danish press, when American newspapers declined to publish them for fear of reprisals, and when the U.S. State Department condemned their publication. The ACLU press office even advised ducking questions about them that arose during discussions of torture at Abu Ghraib. Official talking points recommended responding to questions about the cartoons by exhorting the U.S. government to "demonstrate . . . that it is taking the Abu Ghraib images seriously." (This was later spun as an effort to stay on message about abuses at Abu Ghraib.)

Not until an ACLU donor complained about this silence on the cartoon controversy, and questions about it were raised before the ACLU board, did Romero address it—quietly. He mentioned the controversy in a relatively obscure dinner speech to the National Association of Hispanic Journalists. He sent a letter to the University of Illinois urging it not to discipline student editors who published the cartoons in a campus paper. In a widely circulated e-mail to the concerned donor, Romero both denied and defended the ACLU's relative silence: "With regard to the cartoons, rather than put out a hortatory statement that no one would read (except insiders) but might make us feel good about ourselves, we have tried to engage in thoughtful forums and discussions that relate to the issue. Speaking out on an issue involves more than slapping a paragraph together and posting it on a website." Undoubtedly. The ACLU's public relations campaigns exemplify the inadequacies of "hortatory statements" in defense of liberty. Whatever Romero's reasons for staying out of the cartoon controversy, they did not include disdain for paying lip service to free speech.

"ACLU Defends Nazi's Right to Burn Down ACLU Headquarters," the humor magazine the *Onion* announced in 1999.[25] Those of us who loved the ACLU, and celebrated its willingness to defend the rights of Nazis and others who had no regard for our rights, considered the joke a compliment. Today it's more like a reproach. Once the nation's leading civil liberties group and reliable defender of everyone's speech rights, the ACLU is becoming just another liberal human-rights, social-justice advocate that reliably defends the rights of liberal speakers.

Conservative speakers are hardly defenseless. They have their own advocacy groups, like the Alliance Defense Fund, which is devoted to defending the speech and associational rights of religious conservatives. But the rise of organizations dedicated to preserving the speech rights of their political allies is not a victory but a defeat for liberty. Civil liberty depends on preserving fair, neutral standards and processes that protect all speech equally, regardless of content or political bias. Conservative organizations that protect the rights of conservative speakers and liberal organizations that protect the rights of liberal speakers—or people who don't deeply offend liberals—advance a perversely partisan, result-oriented ethic of rights that is anathema to liberty.

9

Going It Alone

Threaten the liberty of individuals and you threaten the character and competence of their collectives. Whether legal or social, formal or informal, repression doesn't simply deprive groups of the ideas that dissent may inspire or provide; it also deprives individuals of the opportunity to develop ideas and the willingness to voice them in dissent. Bereft of liberty, John Stuart Mill wrote, people learn to "imitate," but not to choose, or think. "Human liberty . . . comprises, first, the inward domain of consciousness, demanding liberty of conscience, in the most comprehensive sense, liberty of thought and feeling, absolute freedom of opinion and sentiment on all subjects, practical or speculative, scientific, moral, or theological. . . . The human faculties of perception, judgment, discriminative feeling, mental activity, and even moral preference are exercised only in making a choice." Bereft of liberty, people are bereft of "character."[1]

If individuals lack character then so will their communities. This little truism is obvious but often overlooked when civil libertarianism is confused with solipsism, and hostility to majority rule wrongly equated with hostility to communal welfare. Of course, particular exercises of individual rights sometimes conflict with particular communal preferences or interests. But in general, as Mill observed, societies benefit "for containing many persons who have much character."[2]

The relationships between individualism, communal action, and communal ethics are complex. Think of Rosa Parks refusing to take her place at the back of the bus, asserting both her own individual integrity and her membership in a social movement that challenged prevailing laws and customs. Parks and other civil rights activists of the 1950s and '60s were lawbreakers, but they were also moral exemplars, engaged in a struggle to implement constitutional ideals of liberty and equality. By being true to themselves, civil rights activists persuaded the nation to be truer to itself. They had the courage of its professed convictions.

The civil rights movement is a simple, uncontroversial example of virtuous dissent and disobedience, given the now widely acknowledged immorality of the system it dismantled. But consensus about the righteousness of a protest movement can take decades to develop; we're more often challenged to recognize the value of protests we strongly oppose: in recent years, abortion-rights advocates have repeatedly tried to limit the speech rights of antiabortion activists, with occasional success. (The Supreme Court struck down efforts to apply anti-extortion and racketeering laws to antiabortion groups but has upheld some limits on the right to protest outside abortion clinics.)[3] The legal battle over these protests has been complicated by violence against abortion providers, but occasional acts of violence by some members of a movement or group is not a just or legal basis for denying the rights of all members: the Supreme Court also struck down efforts to hold the National Association for the Advancement of Colored People (NAACP) liable for occasional acts of violence during a prolonged civil rights–era boycott of white merchants in Mississippi.[4] Whether or not peaceful antiabortion protesters rightly compare themselves to civil rights activists of the 1960s, reproductive-choice advocates wrongly seek to deny their right to protest peacefully outside abortion clinics. Protected acts of conscience can hardly be limited to those that you, or the majority, endorse, while those you oppose are dismissed as wrongful disruptions of justifiable collective order.

Advocates on both sides of the abortion debate occasionally seek "common ground," but their essential moral differences are absolute: whether abortion prohibitions are justifiable deprivations of female autonomy or equality depends almost entirely on whether abortion is considered homicide. First Amendment values and rights are essential to negotiating conflicts between nonnegotiable differences like this. Choosing freedom of speech, thought, and association, and freedom from or for religion over the truth of any particular set of beliefs, civil libertarianism is, in part, a procedural response to the clash of absolutes.

Civil disobedience chooses sides, in dramatic, public assertions of individual conscience. But whether individuals defy public laws or the private rules and mores of their groups, they elevate their own instincts or judgments over the decisions of their collectives. By what authority? Religious teachings are obvious and common sources of authority, and, to the frustration of nontheists, conventional wisdom holds that belief in God is essential to virtue. Recognizing no absolute, divine authorities, nontheists are suspected of playing by their own rules for their own advantages. Secularists inspire similar mistrust, although secularism is a theory of civics, not metaphysics: belief in godless government does not preclude belief in God; but opposing church/state partnerships and public policies reflective of religious faiths, secularists, like nontheists, would deprive government of what some consider essential moral guidance. Confronted with assumptions about their essential immorality, humanists anxiously issue manifestos affirming their "ability and responsibility to lead ethical lives . . . guided by reason, inspired by compassion, and informed by experience."[5] Transcendentalists and their descendants, eschewing organized religion and atheism, choose a third way, putting their faith in a unifying, divine Whatever, with which they might successfully, if momentarily, commune: "We lie in the lap of immense intelligence, which makes us receivers of its truth and organs of its activity," Emerson explained. "When we discern justice, when we discern truth, we do nothing ourselves, but allow a passage to its beams." There was no use in asking "whence this comes"; "Its presence or absence is all we can affirm."[6]

But no religious, spiritual, or humanist rhetoric about metaphysical, moral dictates or realities is likely to resonate with people who aren't already prone to regard it as true. Abstractions about ethics or morality function less like arguments capable of persuasion or conversion than as confirmations of what people already believe, or intuit, with varying degrees of conviction. Moral absolutism and moral relativism are stereotypically viewed as partisan attributes; absolutists supposedly occupy the right and relativists the left. But we're all relativists, and we're all absolutists, depending on the issue, regardless of the authority for our beliefs. We tend to dismiss people as moralistic or accuse them of judgmentalism when they make judgments with which we disagree or about matters we regard as morally neutral. You say tomato and I say tomahto. Pronunciation preferences are morally irrelevant. Do sexual preferences raise moral questions? Should abortion or assisted suicide be permissible? There we vehemently disagree. Whether moral dogmatism is a vice or virtue, it's shared by people of various and often opposing political and religious beliefs. That's why we've had a culture war. If all the absolutists were arrayed on one side and all the relativists on the other, the absolutists would have won by default long ago.

For my own practical purposes, questions about the source or inspiration of my ideals (or anyone else's) are usually moot (and I leave them to theologians, philosophers, and scientists). No deities or prophets speak to me. Neither does the universe. I give religion no general credit for virtue and impose on it no general blame for vice. With or without belief in God, people act badly; with or without belief in God, people act well (although perhaps with less reliability). I tend to blame human nature for the evils that some religionists attribute to atheism and some atheists attribute to religion. I tend to rely on the moral authority of instinct, which is another way of saying that I believe in the dictates of my own conscience, regardless of how they've been shaped, even though I don't always manage to obey them. This is obviously an individualistic approach to morality, but it is not unmitigated moral relativism. Even if I can point to no objective, higher authority, I remain convinced that sometimes in moral disputes, I am right and others are wrong (as this book probably indicates). This doesn't make me an absolutist, but it does mean that I am sometimes willing to act like one, relatively speaking.

Uncertainty about the authority of conscience is a poor excuse for ignoring its demands or imposing special limits on the right to act on them. Occasionally the law defers to individual conscience, most notably in granting conscientious-objector status to people opposed to war, and this deference to conscience must be indiscriminate: to qualify as a conscientious objector, your pacifism need not be based in religious belief, the Supreme Court ruled some forty years ago; it may reflect a deeply held, secular moral ideal.[7]

The selective-service-law exemption for conscientious objectors doesn't just benefit dissenting individuals; it's of great value, as well, to "the democratic community at large," the Supreme Court observed.[8] "Liberty of conscience" has both "moral and social value," the Court stressed. Protecting it is "sound policy . . . nothing short of the self-preservation of the state should warrant its violation; and it may well be questioned whether the state which preserves its life by a settled policy of violation of the conscience of the individual will not in fact ultimately lose it by the process."[9] In other words, individual acts of conscience are protected partly because they protect the community.

Individual-conscience exemptions to generally applicable laws are not common (although exemptions for religious groups have expanded greatly in the past ten years), but when the law provides no conscience clause, you still have the option of defying it, and your defiance arguably benefits the community too. Breaking what you regard as an unjust law and submitting to punishment may or may not be an altruistic act exactly, depending on its motivation, but it is often a socially enlightening one. Civil disobedience does not simply reflect the elevation of individual conscience over communal law; it represents an appeal by the individual to the communal conscience, an insistence on ideals that the law discarded or forgot. It requires both individualism and a sense of community—even a negative sense of community will do. Henry David Thoreau disdained society, preferring the pleasure, or challenge, of his own company, yet his classic formulation of civil disobedience reflects an acute awareness of individual responsibility for collective sin.

Thoreau was a man of inaction: neither activist nor reformer, he recognized no particular obligation to remedy wrongs; but he was driven by a strong desire not to be complicit in them. "I came into this world not chiefly to make this a good place to live in, but to live in it, be it good or bad," he wrote. "What I have to do is to see, at any rate, that I do not lend myself to the wrong which I condemn."[10] The monstrous wrong of his day was slavery, and while Thoreau did not take action against it (unlike John Brown, whom he eulogized), he famously refused to pay taxes to the Commonwealth of Massachusetts because it belonged to a Union that included slaveholding states and respected the legal prerogatives of slaveholders. (He spent only a night in jail because someone paid his taxes for him, with no thanks from Thoreau.)

His effort to disaffiliate from the commonwealth was a reflection of temperament as well as political conviction, not surprisingly. He inclined toward isolationism, regarding what is exalted today as "social networking" most skeptically. "Ordinary conversation" was "hollow and ineffectual," Thoreau wrote. "Surface meets surface. When our life ceases to be inward and private, conversation degenerates into mere gossip."[11] He described his "connection with and obligation to society" as "very slight and transient."[12] Thoreau not only avoided enlisting in groups; he actively sought exclusion from them, as political theorist Nancy Rosenblum has stressed: "He was uncomfortably unable to name all of the societies he had never joined but that nonetheless claimed his loyalty and imposed their obligations, and he repeatedly disavowed affiliation."[13] Thoreau doubted the wisdom of crowds. "There is but little virtue in the actions of masses of men," he declared.[14]

He was of a type described by Emerson in his portrait of transcendentalists: "It is a sign of our times . . . that many intelligent and religious persons withdraw themselves from the common labors and competitions of the market and the caucus, and betake themselves to a certain solitary and critical way of living, from which solid fruit has yet appeared to justify their separation. . . . They are lonely; the spirit of their writing and conversation is lonely; they repel influences; they shun general society; they incline to shut themselves in their chamber in the house, to live in the country rather than in the town, and to find their tasks and amusements in solitude." Naturally, as Emerson noted, they were "not good citizens, not good members of society; unwillingly they bear their part of the public and private burdens. . . . They do not even like to vote."[15]

This was a spiritual stance (and for some, no doubt, a spiritual pose). Shielded from the demands and distractions of commerce or philanthropy, the transcendentalists to whom Emerson paid tribute were blessed or cursed with "moments of illumination" that left them with little use or tolerance for social, political, or commercial endeavors. This was a philosophy that could serve as an excuse for self-indulgence, or a mandate for self-discipline. Taken seriously, it reflected an unyielding, introspective quest for perfection. The solitary transcendentalists made "extravagant demands on human nature," Emerson observed. "They are the most exacting and extortionate critics. . . . They pay you only this one compliment of insatiable expectation."[16]

I don't posit Thoreau as the model citizen for an ethical democracy, which obviously requires active participants and joiners. I don't share his taste for solitude (or his distaste for gossip and ability to resist it). I don't endorse his pessimism about collective endeavors, although I am sympathetic to it. And while Thoreau didn't model citizenship, he did challenge it with essential ideals—his "extravagant demands" and "insatiable expectations." Social psychologists provide explanations and predictions of cruel, cowardly, or conformist group behavior; Thoreau offers an antidote for it—a vision of individual integrity forged in solitude that can survive the pressures of social relations.

An effective association of radical or romantic individualists is as difficult to imagine as an effective association of anarchists. Yet I suspect that virtually every association can benefit from the presence of at least a few individualists who are willing and able to defy their fellow members. Some are natural-born dissenters; some become dissenters by default. Temperament, character, and circumstance (especially financial independence) obviously help determine how people react to collective corruption (and character may only reveal itself when people are under stress). Predicting who will collaborate, actively or passively, in unethical behavior and who will try to subvert or openly challenge it is surprisingly difficult. But quirky people, oddballs who aren't likely to become part of the elite, are more likely to stand up to the group and challenge its dominant majority than people with hopes of advancing in the group hierarchy. Outliers are less likely to have internalized the popular view, and have so much less to lose by challenging it. The integrity of groups often depends perversely on providing openings for members to whom the group has been the least welcoming and on the inclusion of members with a temperamental antipathy toward group behavior—individualists who have perhaps joined the group partly in spite of themselves.

Virtually all of us have succumbed to social pressures and deferred to collective judgments, on occasion at least; and that is not always lamentable. I don't mean to denigrate our social instincts, collegiality, or cooperation, and I take for granted that groups are sometimes smarter than individuals. But I suspect that groups are smartest when members retain their individuality and faith in their own judgments, distinguishing between cooperation and co-option, wending their ways between radical individualism and immersion in the collective. So while I don't mean to romanticize contrarianism or to characterize individualism as an unmitigated good, I regard them as oddly essential to associational life. People drawn to identify with groups aren't likely to be tempted by individualism's vices. Perhaps they might learn from its virtues.

Acknowledgments

I'm deeply grateful to my always patient editor, Helene Atwan, and most admiring of her intelligence, integrity, and courage. Many thanks to Jane Isay, whose unerring instincts and vision helped shape this book, and to Nancy Rosenblum and Janet Fries, for their generosity in reviewing the manuscript.

Notes

1. Mob Scenes

1. It would be a waste of the reader's time and mine for me to review findings that have been so clearly explained and summarized by others. For a primer on social psychology, see Elliot Aronson, ed., *Readings about the Social Animal,* 9th ed. (New York: Worth Publishers, 2003). See also Irving L. Janis, *Groupthink: Psychological Studies of Policy Decisions and Fiascoes,* 2nd ed. (Boston: Houghton Mifflin, 1982). And for an insightful essay on dissent that draws from social psychology, see Cass R. Sunstein, *Why Societies Need Dissent* (Cambridge, Mass.: Harvard University Press, 2003).

2. In the early twentieth century, Emma Goldman and Eugene Debs were imprisoned for opposing the draft during World War I. The Sedition Act of 1918 prohibited criticism of the government. Extensively examined red scares of the 1920s, '40s, and '50s employed formal and informal means of punishing or chilling dissent.

3. Quoted in Bryan Keefer, "Closing Down Debate: Ashcroft's Attack on Dissent," Spinsanity.org, December 10, 2001: www.spinsanity .org/columns/20011210.html.

4. Thomas P. Doyle, A. W. Richard Sipe, and Patrick J. Wall, *Sex, Priests, and Secret Codes: The Catholic Church's 2,000-Year Paper Trail of Sexual Abuse* (Los Angeles: Volt Press, 2006); Investigative Staff of the *Boston Globe, Betrayal: The Crisis in the Catholic Church* (Boston: Little, Brown, 2002).

2. The Problem with Partisanship

1. Stephanie Strom, "ACLU Will Consider Disciplining 2 Officials," *New York Times,* January 21, 2005.

2. This is not a comprehensive exposé of all our controversies, which would be too tedious to read or write, but I and a few others are in the process of making a comprehensive record available for study in a pub-

licly accessible archive, to be announced on the Beacon Press Web site, at http://www.beacon.org/worstinstincts. I have relied on this record of internal e-mails, tapes, and minutes of meetings, and various documents—memos, press releases, fundraising appeals, and policy proposals—throughout this book. I have not supplied notes for many of these references (partly because they are not yet publicly accessible) but have simply cited their provenance in the text.

3. *ACLU v. NSA,* 128 S. Ct. 1334 (2007); *Amnesty International USA et al. v. McConnell et al.,* see www.aclu.org/pdfs/safefree/faa_complaint_20080710.pdf.

4. I realize that, by referencing private conversations with staff members who insist on anonymity, I am asking readers to trust assertions that I cannot document, and I regret not being able to identify my sources. Still, I consider them worth citing (and have done so on a few occasions throughout the book), understanding that some readers will ignore or discount their remarks. I don't need these sources to make my case; the material facts on which I rely are documented or otherwise corroborated. But I do want to pay tribute to those staff members who've tried to do their jobs, at times against the odds.

5. Shortly after the Save the ACLU Web site appeared, Gara La-Marche, then vice president and director of U.S. programs at the Open Society Institute, sent an e-mail to leaders of other organizations inviting them to sign a letter of support for the ACLU leadership: "I think that what the ACLU leadership is going through right now requires solidarity from those of us who support the organization and believe it is doing a vitally effective job at a critical time," LaMarche stressed, concluding with his official OSI signature. (LaMarche is now CEO and president of the Atlantic Philanthropies.)

6. Benedict Carey, "Denial Makes the World Go Round," *New York Times,* November 20, 2007.

7. Shankar Vedantam, "Persistence of Myths Could Alter Public Policy Approach," *Washington Post,* September 4, 2007.

8. Zogby International, "9/11 + 5 Reveals Dramatic Partisan Split," September 5, 2006, www.zogby.com/news/ReadNews.dbm?ID=1169.

9. Peggy Noonan, "Pity Party," *Wall Street Journal,* May 16, 2008.

3. Not the Crime but the Cover-up

1. ACLU Letter to FTC Re: Eli Lilly, July 5, 2001, www.aclu.org/privacy/medical/15372res20010705.html.

2. Robert O'Harrow Jr., "ACLU Admits Another Privacy Gaffe: Names, E-Mail Addresses of Hundreds Sent over Internet," *Washington Post,* February 26, 2003.

3. Jeffrey A. Sonnenfeld, "What Makes Great Boards Great," *Harvard Business Review* (September 2002), pp. 106–13.

4. David France, "Freedom to Backstab," *New York Magazine*, February 12, 2007, www.nymag.com/news/features/27839.

5. While we were debating Romero's handling of the consent agreement, several board members privately observed that he was nobly taking the heat for one of his staffers, on whose bad advice he had relied. It didn't seem to occur to them that if Romero were actually taking the heat for a staffer, he would be careful not to advertise the fact. Eventually, Romero would publicly blame a subordinate for the failure to distribute the consent agreement: "Barry read it wrong," he remarked rather cravenly to a reporter. See France, "Freedom to Backstab."

6. My account of this call is based on a report by Michael Meyers, who participated in the call and subsequently listened to a tape of it made by Romero and kept in the ACLU office.

7. ACLU Policy 518, "Disclosure of ACLU Information."

8. Susan Gross's presentation was recorded and also summarized in minutes of the November 22, 2003, executive committee meeting (which I attended and described in a memo to the national board).

9. Dennis Thompson, *Restoring Responsibility: Ethics in Government, Business, and Healthcare* (Cambridge: Cambridge University Press, 2005), pp. 248–49, 253.

4. The Political Shouldn't Be Personal

1. Jay W. Lorsch and Alison H. Watson, *The United Way of America: Governance in the Nonprofit Sector (A)* (Cambridge, Mass.: Harvard Business School, October 12, 1993), p. 8.

2. This was a private conversation, and Herman may deny that it occurred or contradict my account of it. Generally, I've relied on documented facts and comments in telling this story, but I've made a few exceptions and describe Herman's unrecorded remarks because they're so revealing of the personal dynamics that compromised the executive committee's ability to provide oversight.

I don't pretend to have verbatim recall of her comments, but I do recall them quite clearly, mainly because they were so startling. We spoke at the October 2003 board meeting, shortly after the board concluded a two-hour discussion of the consent-agreement controversy. Another highly respected board leader, Diane Geraghty, a law professor at Loyola University, had mentioned to me privately that most members of the executive committee privately considered my critique of Romero's conduct "more right than wrong." I replied that they ought to say as much to me, and about five minutes later, Herman pulled me aside for this private conversation, in which she explained why she overlooked what she tacitly acknowledged were Romero's lies.

3. Morisey's grievance was a confidential filing. She subsequently described it briefly to the board only after the lawyers against whom it was filed had described it.

4. Nancy L. Rosenblum, *Membership and Morals: The Personal Uses of Pluralism in America* (Princeton, N.J.: Princeton University Press, 1998), pp. 8–9, 360–61.

5. Barry Newman, "Fans of Dr. Forni Spread Civility," *Wall Street Journal,* April 5, 2008.

6. Jeré Longman, "U.S. Goalkeeper Faces Difficult Save," *New York Times,* May 25, 2008.

7. Dennis Thompson, *Restoring Responsibility: Ethics in Government, Business, and Healthcare* (Cambridge: Cambridge University Press, 2005), pp. 300, 303.

8. Ibid., p. 303.

9. Ibid., pp. 303–4.

5. Facts Don't Matter

1. Warren Buffett, Berkshire Hathaway Inc., 2002 Annual Report, pp. 10–11.

2. Jeffrey A. Sonnenfeld, "What Makes Great Boards Great," *Harvard Business Review* (September 2002), p. 111.

3. Stephanie Strom, "ACLU's Search for Data on Donors Stirs Privacy Fears," *New York Times,* December 18, 2004.

4. Ibid.

5. ACLU Policy 272, "Government Data Collection, Storage, and Dissemination," par. B, "By Commercial Entities."

6. ACLU Policy 528, "Free Speech for ACLU Employees and Lay Leaders."

7. Elliot Aronson, ed., *Readings about the Social Animal,* 9th ed. (New York: Worth Publishers, 2003), p. 17.

8. Solomon Asch, "Opinions and Social Pressure," in *Readings About the Social Animal,* ed. Aronson, pp. 17–26, 25.

9. Howard F. Stein, "Organizational Totalitarianism and the Voices of Dissent," *Journal of Organizational Psychodynamics* 1, no. 1 (spring 2007), pp. 8, 9, 11.

10. Howard S. Schwartz, "Narcissism Project and Corporate Decay: The Case of General Motors," *Business Ethics Quarterly* 1, no. 3 (1991), pp. 249–54.

11. Statement of James Ferguson, www.savetheaclu.org/?cat=8.

12. Schwartz, "Narcissism Project and Corporate Decay," p. 258.

13. Schwartz, "Organizational Disaster and Organizational Decay: The Case of the National Aeronautics and Space Administration," *Industrial Crisis Quarterly* 3 (1989), pp. 319–34.

14. Gene Healy, "The Cult of the Presidency," *Reason,* June 2008, www.reason.com/news/show/126020.html.

15. Mark Leibovich, "Where to Catch the Sights, Sound and Smell of a Campaign," *New York Times,* May 24, 2008.

16. Athena Jones, "Clinton Rallies Pa. Women," March 24, 2008, http://firstread.msnbc.msn.com/archive/2008/03.aspx.

6. Money Changes Everything

1. *National Nonprofit Ethics Survey: An Inside View of Nonprofit Sector Ethics* (Arlington, VA: Ethics Resource Center, 2007).

2. This account is excerpted from Ira Glasser's final, January 2001 budget memo to the ACLU national board.

3. I have contributed to the ACLU's endowment, the Trust for the Bill of Rights, which my husband helped launch.

4. *Brandenburg v. Ohio,* 395 U.S. 444 (1969).

5. Daniel Goldin, "Colleges Object To New Wording in Ford Grants," *Wall Street Journal,* May 4, 2004.

6. Transcript, ACLU executive committee meeting, May 22, 2004.

7. Minutes, ACLU Foundation board conference call, June 7, 2004.

8. Ford issued its new grant restrictions after coming under pressure from members of Congress (right and left), notably former Republican senator Rick Santorum and New York congressman Jerrold Nadler. It was also the subject of scathing articles in the Jewish Telegraphic Agency, a pro-Israel wire service. See, generally, Scott Sherman, "Target Ford," *Nation,* June 5, 2006.

9. Digital recording, ACLU executive committee meeting, August 7, 2004. With the support of the executive committee, Romero had refused to answer written questions that I submitted in June 2004 about his involvement in formulating the Ford Foundation grant restrictions; but at the August 2004 executive committee meeting, after the grant restrictions had been approved by the board, Susan Herman read my questions out loud and Romero volunteered to answer them.

10. Stephanie Strom, "ACLU Rejects Foundation Grants Over Terror Language," *New York Times,* October 19, 2004.

11. Adam Liptak, "ACLU Board Is Split Over Terror Watch Lists," *New York Times,* July 31, 2004.

12. OMB Watch and Grantmakers without Borders, *Collateral Damage: How the War on Terror Hurts Charities, Foundations, and the People They Serve,* July 14, 2008. (This report misleadingly praises the ACLU for protesting Ford Foundation grant restrictions, without noting Romero's role in crafting them or the ACLU board's initial decision to approve them, and also avoids acknowledging Romero's embarrassing approval of CFC watch-list requirements; see pp. 45–47.)

13. A synopsis of the complicated history of *Humanitarian Law Project et al. v. Mukasey et al.* can be found on the Web site of the Center for Constitutional Rights: see http://ccrjustice.org/ourcases/current-cases/humanitarian-law-project%2C-et-al.-v.-mukasey%2C-hlp%2C-et-al.-v.-gonzales%2C-and-hlp.

14. Liptak, "ACLU Board Is Split Over Terror Watch Lists."

15. Digital recording and minutes, ACLU executive committee meeting, August 7, 2004.

16. OMB Watch and Grantmakers without Borders, *Collateral Damage*; Lawyers' Committee for Civil Rights of the San Francisco Bay Area, "The OFAC List: How a Treasury Department Terrorist Watchlist Ensnares Everyday Consumers," March 2007, www.lccr.com/03%202007%20OFAC%20Report.pdf.

17. Digital recording, ACLU executive committee meeting, August 7, 2004.

18. The counsel letter is privileged, arguably. Romero may have waived the privilege when he described or pretended to describe its contents. He clearly waived privilege as to the provisions that he mischaracterized, as my attorneys advise me. Counsel's opinion letter, dated July 30, 2004, stated:

> While the most prudent course of action to ensure compliance would be to cross-check the ACLU's personnel list and list of organizations to whom the ACLU contributes against the lists referenced in the certification, an alternative reasonable interpretation would only require that the ACLU not know or have reason to know that an employee or organization receiving ACLU funds is on one of the terrorist/international criminal lists.

But, the letter continued,

> The ACLU and the individual signatory by signing the certification have acknowledged the existence of the terrorists lists and by confirming that they do not knowingly contribute or employ any listed individual or entity, there is strong implication that they know the contents of those lists.

It concluded rather ominously:

> Thus, by signing the certification requirement in the context of not comparing employees or donees with the relevant lists, the ACLU and the individual signing the certification on behalf of the ACLU may expose themselves to criminal liability for knowingly making a false statement to the United States. . . . Finally, the simple act of signing the certification form may

be used by the government to prove that the ACLU and the individual signatory had the requisite knowledge in a prosecution against the ACLU for "knowingly provid[ing] material support" to a foreign terrorist organization . . . signing the certification statement alone may constitute sufficient proof of "knowledge" such that a conviction against the signatory of the certification may be sustained.

19. Scott Sherman, "ACLU v. ACLU," *Nation*, February 5, 2007.

20. The only motion involving the CFC that the board passed at its July 9, 2004, meeting simply required the executive director to report back in October 2004 on the meaning and effect of restrictions imposed by three funders, the CFC and the Charles Stewart Mott and MacArthur foundations.

7. Potemkin Villages

1. Lawyers' Committee for Civil Rights of the San Francisco Bay Area, "The OFAC List: How a Treasury Department Terrorist Watchlist Ensnares Everyday Consumers," March 2007, www.lccr.com/03% 202007%20OFAC%20Report.pdf.

2. *Humanitarian Law Project et al. v. Mukasey et al.*, http://ccrjustice .org/ourcases/current-cases/humanitarian-law-project%2C-et-al.-v.-mukasey%2C-hlp%2C-et-al.-v.-gonzales%2C-and-hlp.

3. *American Civil Liberties Union et al. v. United States Office of Personnel Management*, www.aclu.org/FilesPDFs/cfc_complaint.pdf.

4. David J. Craig, "Legal Combatant," *Columbia Magazine* (winter 2006/2007), pp. 25–31.

5. Romero had planned an elaborate press conference to announce the Guantánamo initiative, but the *Wall Street Journal* broke the story first. See Jess Bravin, "ACLU to Back Up Defense of 9/11 Detainees," April 4, 2008.

6. Denny LeBoeuf, a dedicated capital-defense attorney, became director of the John Adams Project in August 2008. LeBoeuf and I were friends (although I avoided discussing ACLU matters with her), and I greatly respect her commitment to capital defense. I hold Romero (and the national board) responsible for the misleading marketing of the John Adams Project, not the attorneys involved in it.

7. Bravin, "ACLU to Back Up Defense of 9/11 Detainees." See also William Glaberson and Neil A. Lewis, "2 Groups to Help Defend Detainees at Guantánamo," *New York Times*, April 4, 2008.

8. See "ACLU of Texas Observing FLDS Custody Hearings in San Angelo," www.aclutx.org/article.php?aid=568. The ACLU was criticized for not speaking up sooner, so it's not entirely surprising that

the date on this press release is conspicuously absent (at least it was when I last checked in October 2008). But other press reports (and my own records) confirm that it issued on April 18, 2008. See, for example, Randy Sly, "ACLU on the FLDS and Child Custody," www.catholic.org/national/nation_story.php?id=27675.

9. *In re Texas Department of Family and Protective Services*, 51 Tex. Sup. J. 967 (2008).

10. *In re Sara Steed et al.*, 2008 Tex. App. LEXIS 3652.

11. See American Civil Liberties Union of Massachusetts, Annual Report 2007, www.aclum.org/2007/ACLUM_Annual_Report_2007.pdf, p. 8.

12. ACLU statement on YFZ Ranch, May 2, 2008, www.aclutx.org/aricle.php?aid=570.

13. *In re Texas Department of Family and Protective Services*, brief of amici curiae in opposition to relator's petition for mandamus, May 29, 2008, www.aclu.org/religion/gen/35467lgl20080529.html.

14. Howard F. Schwartz, "Narcissism Project and Corporate Decay: The Case of General Motors," *Business Ethics Quarterly* 1, no. 3 (1991), pp. 255, 259.

15. Again, the staff members I've quoted here were wary of speaking out and insisted on complete anonymity, so I can't disclose anything that might identify them. I understand that some readers may not want to take these remarks on faith.

16. Schwartz, "Narcissism Project and Corporate Decay," p. 263.

8. Gag Rules

1. Josh Gerstein, "Maloney May Lose ACLU in Fight on Abortion," *New York Sun,* April 11, 2006.

2. Stephanie Strom, "ACLU May Block Criticism by Its Board," *New York Times,* May 24, 2006.

3. Ibid.

4. Vassar College Regulations 07/08, "Academic Freedom and Responsibility," excerpted at Foundation for Individual Rights in Education, www.thefire.org/index.php/codes/1155.

5. "'Freedom Is About Authority': Excerpts from Giuliani Speech on Crime," *New York Times,* March 20, 1994.

6. See Emily Guidry, "More Commentary on *New York Times* Piece," June 29, 2007, www.thefire.org/index.php/article/8186.html; and Greg Lukianoff, "*New York Times* Disappoints," www.thefire.org/index.php/article/8185.html.

7. John Stuart Mill, *On Liberty,* ed. Gertrude Himmelfarb (Harmondsworth, U.K.: Penguin, 1985), p. 151.

8. Quoted in Jim Brown, "FIRE Blasts Johns Hopkins for Letting

Conservative Paper Be Censored," *Agape Press,* June 19, 2006, www
.thefire.org/index.php/article/7124.html.

9. Examples of campus censorship abound. At the University of
Delaware, a mandatory orientation program sought to rid students
of presumptively incorrect self-images and views about race, sex, sex-
uality, and politics, replacing them with official orthodoxies, like the
belief that all white people are racists. (This program was terminated
after a spate of bad publicity and perhaps the realization of administrators that the University of Delaware was a public institution, liable
to be sued by students for violating their First Amendment rights.) At
Northeastern University, students are prohibited from using university
information systems to transmit any material deemed "offensive . . . in
the sole judgment of the university." At Tufts University, a conservative
magazine was found guilty of harassment for publishing articles mocking affirmative action and Islamic fundamentalism. See www.thefire
.org for descriptions of these and many other cases.

See also Greg Lukianoff, "Campus Speech Codes: Absurd, Tena-
cious, and Everywhere," May 23, 2008, National Association of Schol-
ars, www.nas.org/polArticles.cfm?Doc_Id=190.

10. Vanessa E. Jones, "They're Sitting Right Next to Us," *Boston
Globe,* December 5, 2007.

11. Mill, *On Liberty,* p. 77.

12. Nadine Strossen, *Defending Pornography: Free Speech, Sex, and the
Fight for Women's Rights* (New York: New York University Press, 2000),
pp. 21, 25, 128–9, 130.

13. Ibid., p. 125.

14. Clyde Haberman, "In Noble Campaign against a Slur, Reasons
for Pause," *New York Times,* February 27, 2007.

15. *McCullen et al. v. Coakley.* The ACLU of Massachusetts planned
to submit an amicus brief opposing the buffer zone after ADF lost its
case in district court and filed an appeal.

16. *Harper v. Poway Unified Sch. Dist.,* 127 S. Ct. 1484 (2007). For
a brief summary of the case, see www.firstamendmentcenter.org/fac
library/case.aspx?case=Harper_v_Poway_Unified_School_District&
SearchString=poway.

17. *Morse v. Frederick,* 127 S. Ct. 2618 (2007).

18. "ACLU Announces Winners of 2007 Youth Activist Scholarship," April 19, 2007, www.aclu.org/students/29364prs20070419.html.

19. "ACLU Secures Promise from Missouri High School to Stop
Censoring Student's Gay-Supportive T-Shirts," June 23, 2005, www
.aclu.org/lgbt/youth/12249prs20050623.html.

20. *Harper v. Poway Unified Sch. Dist.,* 445 F.3d 1166 (2006).

21. I wrote about the *Harper v. Poway* case in a *Wall Street Journal*

op-ed, in which some of the discussion here first appeared. See Wendy Kaminer, "The American Liberal Liberties Union," *Wall Street Journal,* May 23, 2007.

22. *Sklar v. Clough,* Memorandum of Law of Amici Curiae ACLU and ACU of Georgia in support of Neither Party on plaintiff's motion for preliminary injunction, June 20, 2006.

23. See FIRE's amicus brief in *Dejohn v. Temple University,* www .thefire.org/pdfs/3cba9b5d84e4fd5c96cd402873f8a6f7.pdf.

24. Stephanie Strom, "ACLU May Block Criticism by Its Board," *New York Times,* May 24, 2006.

25. "ACLU Defends Nazis' Right to Burn Down ACLU Headquarters," October 14, 2003, www.theonion.com/content/node/39182.

9. Going It Alone

1. John Stuart Mill, *On Liberty,* ed. Gertrude Himmelfarb (Harmondsworth, U.K.: Penguin, 1985), pp. 71, 122–25.

2. Ibid., p. 125.

3. *Scheidler et al. v. National Organization for Women, Inc., et al.,* 547 U.S. 9 (2006); *Hill v. Colorado,* 530 U.S. 703 (2000).

4. *NAACP v. Claiborne Hardware,* 458 U.S. 886 (1982).

5. Humanist Manifesto III, www.americanhumanist.org/3/Hum andItsAspirations.php.

6. Ralph Waldo Emerson, "Self Reliance," *The Essential Writings of Ralph Waldo Emerson,* ed. Brooks Atkinson (New York: Modern Library, 2000), pp. 141–42.

7. *Welsh v. United States,* 398 U.S. 333 (1970).

8. *Gillette v. United States,* 401 U.S. 437, 445 (1971).

9. *United States v. Seeger,* 380 U.S. 163, 170 (1965).

10. Henry David Thoreau, "Civil Disobedience," *Civil Disobedience, and Other Essays* (New York: Dover Publications, 1993), p. 8.

11. Thoreau, "Life without Principle," *Civil Disobedience,* p. 84.

12. Ibid., p. 78.

13. Nancy L. Rosenblum, *Membership and Morals: The Personal Uses of Pluralism in America* (Princeton, N.J.: Princeton University Press, 1998), p. 7.

14. Thoreau, "Civil Disobedience," *Civil Disobedience,* p. 5.

15. Emerson, *The Essential Writings,* pp. 87–90.

16. Ibid., pp. 88–89.